CONVERSATIONS WITH
KAFKA

*

D0870117

19-Curtis Eberhardt-93

CONVERSATIONS WITH

KAFKA

*

Gustav Janouch

translated by Goronwy Rees

*

SECOND EDITION
REVISED AND ENLARGED

A NEW DIRECTIONS BOOK

IN MEMORY OF MY FATHER

*

CONTENTS

✳

CONVERSATIONS WITH KAFKA

*

*

One day at the end of March 1920 my father told me at supper to call on him the following morning at his office.

'I know how often you shirk school to go to the city library,' he said. 'So tomorrow you can come to see me. And dress yourself decently. We shall pay a call.'

I asked him where we were going together.

It seemed to me that my curiosity amused him. But he gave me no explanation.

'Do not ask questions,' he said. 'Don't be inquisitive, and prepare for a surprise.'

The next day when, shortly before midday, I appeared in his office on the third floor of the Workmen's Accident Insurance Institution, he inspected me carefully from top to toe, opened the middle drawer of his desk, took out a green file inscribed *Gustav*, laid it before him and gave me a long look. After a while he said:

'Why are you standing? Take a seat.' The anxious expression on my face provoked a faint mischievous narrowing of his eyelids. 'Don't be afraid, I'm not going to be angry with you,' he began in a friendly manner. 'I want to talk to you as a friend to a friend. Forget that I am your father and listen to me. You write poems.'

He looked at me as if he were going to present me with a bill.

'How do you know?' I stammered. 'How did you find out?'

'It's quite simple,' said my father. 'Each month I get a large electric-light bill. I looked into the reasons for our increased consumption, and I discovered that you have the light on in your room till late at night. I wanted to know what you were doing, and so I kept my eyes open. I found out that you write and write, and always destroy what you have written, or else hide it bashfully in the piano. So one morning when you were in school I took a look at the things.'

'And?'

I swallowed hard.

'And nothing,' said my father. 'I found a black notebook with the title, *The Book of Experience*. 1 was interested. But, all the same, when I discovered it was your diary, I put it aside. I have no desire to ransack your soul.'

'But you read the poems?'

'Yes, those I did read. They were in a dark-coloured portfolio inscribed *The Book of Beauty*. Many of them I could not understand. Some of them I can only describe as stupid.'

'Why did you read them?'

I was seventeen years old, and therefore any intimacy with me was an act of *lèse-majesté*.

'Why should I not read them? Why should I not acquaint myself with your work? I very much wanted to hear a professional opinion by a competent authority. So I had the poems dictated and typewritten in the office.'

'Which of the poems did you copy?'

'All of them,' answered my father. 'I do not respect only what I myself understand. After all, I wanted a criticism not of my taste, but of your work. So I had everything copied and given to Kafka for his opinion.'

'Who is this Kafka? You have never even mentioned him.'

'He's a good friend of Max Brod,' explained my father. 'Max Brod dedicated his novel *Tycho Brache's Way to God* to him.'[1]

'But he is the author of *The Metamorphosis*!' I exclaimed. 'An extraordinary story. Do you know him?'

My father nodded.

'He is in our legal department.'

'What did he say about my poems?'

'He praised them. I thought he was only being polite. But then he asked me to introduce you to him. So I told him that you were coming today.'

'So that is the visit you spoke of.'

'Yes, that is the visit, you scribbler.'

My father conducted me down to the second floor, where we entered a fairly large, well-furnished office.

Behind one of two desks standing side by side sat a tall, slim man. He had black hair combed back, a bony nose, wonderful grey-blue eyes under a strikingly narrow forehead, and bitter-sweet, smiling lips.

'This is certainly he,' he said, instead of greeting us.

'It is,' said my father.

Kafka stretched out his hand to me.

'You needn't be ashamed in front of me. I also have a large electricity bill.'

He laughed, and my shyness vanished.

'So this is the creator of the mysterious bug, Samsa,' I said to myself, disillusioned to see before me a simple, well-mannered man.

'There is too much noise in your poems,' said Franz Kafka, when my father left us alone in the office. 'It is a by-product of youth, which indicates an excess of vitality. So that the noise is itself beautiful, though it has nothing in common with art. On the contrary! The noise mars the expression. But I am no critic, I cannot quickly transform myself into something different, then return to myself and precisely measure the distance. As I said – I am no critic. I am only a man under judgement and a spectator.'

'And the judge?' I asked.

He gave an embarrassed smile.

'Indeed, I am also the usher of the court, yet I do not know the judge. Probably I am quite a humble assistant-usher. I have no definite post.' Kafka laughed.

I laughed with him, though I did not understand him.

'The only definite thing is suffering,' he said earnestly. 'When do you write?'

I was surprised by the question, so I answered quickly:

'In the evening, at night. During the day very rarely. I cannot write during the day.'

'The day is a great enchantment.'

'I am disturbed by the light, the factory, the houses, the windows over the way. Most of all by the light. The light distracts my attention.'

'Perhaps it distracts from the darkness within. It is good when the light overpowers one. If it were not for these horrible sleepless nights, I would never write at all. But they always recall me again to my own dark solitude.'

'Is he not himself the unfortunate bug in *The Metamorphosis*?' I thought.

I was glad when the door opened and my father came in.

*

Kafka has great grey eyes, under thick dark eyebrows. His brown face is very animated. Kafka speaks with his face. Whenever he can substitute for words a movement of his facial muscles, he does so. A smile, contraction of his eyebrows, wrinkling of the narrow forehead, protrusion or pursing of the lips – such movements are a substitute for spoken sentences. Franz Kafka loves gestures, and is therefore economical of them. A gesture of his is not an accompaniment of speech, duplicating the words, but as it were a word from an independent language of movement, a means of communication, thus in no way an involuntary reflex, but a deliberate expression of intention. Folding of the hands, laying of outstretched palms on the surface of his desk, leaning his body back comfortably and yet tensely in his chair, bending his head forward in conjunction with a shrug of the shoulders, pressing his hand to his heart, these are a few of the sparingly used means of expression which he always accompanies with an apologetic smile, as if to say, 'It is true, and I admit, that I am playing a game: yet I hope that my game pleases you. And after all – after all, I only do it to win your understanding for a short while.'

'Kafka is very fond of you,' I said to my father. 'How did you come to know each other?'

'We know each other through the office,' answered my father. 'We first came to know each other better after my sketch for the card-index cabinet. Kafka was very pleased with the model which I made. We began talking, and he told me that in the afternoon after office hours he took lessons from the carpenter Kornhauser in the Poděbradgasse in Karolinenthal. From then on we often talked about personal matters. Then I gave him your poems, and so we became – close acquaintances.'

'Why not friends?'

My father shook his head.

'He is too shy and too reserved for friendship.'

*

On my next visit to Kafka I inquired:

'Do you still go to the carpenter in Karolinenthal?'

'You know about that?'

'My father told me.'

'No, I have not been for a long time. My health does not permit it any more. His Majesty the Body.'

'I can quite understand. Working in a dusty workshop is not very pleasant.'

'There you are wrong. I love to work in workshops. The smell of wood shavings, the humming of saws, the hammer-blows, all enchanted me. The afternoon went so quickly I was always astonished when the evening came.'

'You must certainly have been tired.'

'Tired, but happy. There is nothing more beautiful than some straightforward, concrete, generally useful trade. Apart from carpentry, I have also worked at farming and gardening. It was all much better and worth more than forced labour in the office. There one appears to be something superior, better; but it is only appearance. In reality one is only lonelier and therefore unhappier. That is all. Intellectual labour tears a man out of human society. A craft, on the other hand, leads him towards men. What a pity I can no longer work in the workshop or in the garden.'

'But you would not wish to give up your post?'

'Why not? I have dreamed of going as a farm labourer or an artisan to Palestine.'

'You would leave everything here behind?'

'Everything, if I could make a life that had meaning, stability, and beauty. Do you know the writer Paul Adler?'

'I only know his book *The Magic Flute*.'[2]

'He is in Prague. With his wife and the children.'

'What is his profession?'

'He has none. He has no profession, only a vocation. He travels with his wife and the children from one friend to another. A free man, and a poet. In his presence I always have pangs of conscience, because I allow my life to be frittered away in an office.'

*

In May 1921 I wrote a sonnet which was published by Ludwig Winder in the Sunday supplement of the *Bohemia*.[3]

Kafka said on this occasion:

'You describe the poet as a great and wonderful man whose feet are on the ground, while his head disappears in the clouds. Of course, that is a perfectly ordinary image drawn within the intellectual framework of lower-middle-class convention. It is an illusion based on wish fulfilment, which has nothing in common with reality. In fact, the poet is always much smaller and weaker than the social average. Therefore he feels the burden of earthly existence much more intensely and strongly than other men. For him personally his song is only a scream. Art for the artist is only suffering, through which he releases himself for further suffering. He is not a giant, but only a more or less brightly plumaged bird in the cage of his existence.'

'You too?' I asked.

'I am a quite impossible bird,' said Franz Kafka. 'I am a jackdaw – a *kavka*. The coal merchant in the close of the Tein cathedral has one. Have you seen it?'

'Yes, it flies about outside his shop.'

'Yes, my relative is better off than I am. It is true, of course, that its wings have been clipped. As for me, this was not in any case necessary, as my wings are atrophied. For this reason there are no heights and distances for me. I hop about bewildered among my fellow men. They regard me with deep suspicion.

And indeed I am a dangerous bird, a thief, a jackdaw. But that is only an illusion. In fact, I lack all feeling for shining objects. For that reason I do not even have glossy black plumage. I am grey, like ash. A jackdaw who longs to disappear between the stones. But this is only joking, so that you will not notice how badly things are going with me today.'

I no longer remember how often I visited Franz Kafka in his office. One thing, however, I remember very distinctly: his physical appearance as I – half an hour before the end of office hours – opened the door on the second floor of the Workmen's Accident Insurance Institution.

He sat behind his desk, his head leaning back, legs out-stretched, his hands resting on the desk. Filla's picture, *A Reader of Dostoievsky*, has something of the attitude he assumed. From this point of view, there was a great resemblance between Filla's picture and Kafka's bodily appearance. Yet it was purely external. Behind the outward likeness lay a great inner difference.

Filla's reader was overpowered by something, while Kafka's attitude expressed a voluntary and therefore triumphant sur-render. On the thin lips played a delicate smile, which was much more the reflection of some distant alien joy than an expression of his own happiness. The eyes always looked at people a little from below upwards. Franz Kafka thus had a singular appearance, as if apologizing for being so slender and tall. His entire figure seemed to say, 'I am, forgive me, quite unimpor-tant. You do me a great pleasure, if you overlook me.'

His voice was a hesitating, muted baritone, wonderfully melodious, although it never left the middle range in strength and pitch. Voice, gesture, look, all radiated the peace of under-standing and goodness.

He spoke both Czech and German. But more German. And his German had a hard accent, like that of the German spoken by the Czechs. Yet the likeness is only a faint and inexact one; in fact, they were quite different.

The Czech accent of the German which I am thinking of is harsh. The language sounds as if hacked to pieces. Kafka's speech never made this impression. It seemed angular because of the inner tension: every word a stone. The hardness of his speech was caused by the effort at exactness and precision. It was thus determined by positive personal qualities and not by group characteristics. His speech resembled his hands.

He had large, strong hands, broad palms, thin, fine fingers with flat, spatulate finger-nails and prominent yet very delicate bones and knuckles.

When I remember Kafka's voice, his smile and his hands, I always think of a remark of my father's.

He said, 'Strength combined with scrupulous delicacy: strength, which finds the small things the most difficult.'

*

The office in which Franz Kafka worked was a medium-sized, rather high room, which nevertheless seemed cramped; it had something of the dignified elegance of the senior partner's room in a prosperous firm of solicitors, and it was furnished in the same style. It had two black, polished double doors. One opened into Kafka's office from a dark corridor, crammed with tall filing cabinets and always smelling of stale tobacco smoke and dust. The other, in the middle of the wall to the right of the entrance, led to the other offices at the front of the Workmen's Accident Insurance Institution. To the best of my knowledge, however, this door was never opened. Both visitors and the staff normally used the door from the corridor. They would knock, and Kafka would answer briefly and not very loudly, 'Please!', while his partner who shared the room would bark a curt and bad-tempered 'Come in!'.

The tone of this summons, intended to make the visitor conscious of his insignificance, was in keeping with the permanent frown that knotted the yellow eyebrows, the painful precision of the parting, which ran down to the back of his neck, in the urine-coloured lifeless hair, the high stiff collar with its wide, dark cravat, the high-buttoned waistcoat and slightly protuberant, watery-blue goose eyes of the man who for many years sat opposite to Kafka in his office.

I remember that Franz Kafka always winced slightly at his colleague's peremptory 'Come in!'. He seemed to bend his head and look at the man opposite with unconcealed mistrust, as if expecting a blow. He adopted the same attitude even when his colleague addressed some friendly remark to him. It was clear that there was a painful constraint in Kafka's relations with Treml.

So not long after I had begun to call on him at the Institution I asked: 'Can one speak freely in front of him? Doesn't he perhaps tell tales?'

Kafka shook his head. 'I don't think so. Yet men who worry about their job as much as he does are sometimes capable of very dirty tricks.'

'Are you afraid of him?'

Kafka gave an embarrassed smile. 'The hangman always gets a bad name.'

'What do you mean?'

'The hangman is today a respectable bureaucrat, relatively high up on the civil service pay roll. Why shouldn't there be a hangman concealed in every conscientious bureaucrat?'

'But bureaucrats don't hang anybody!'

'Oh, don't they!' answered Kafka, and brought his hands down sharply on his desk. 'They transform living, changing human beings into dead code numbers, incapable of any change.'

I only answered with a quick nod of the head, because I realized that by generalizing in this way Kafka wanted to avoid any direct discussion of his colleague's character. He was concealing the tension that had existed for years between him and his official working partner. And Treml seemed to realize Kafka's dislike, and so spoke to him *de haut en bas*, both on official and personal matters, in a slightly patronizing manner, with a sarcastic, man-of-the-world smile playing on his thin lips.

Treml's attitude said perfectly plainly: 'I fail to understand why you, the legal adviser to the Institution, should talk to an insignificant sprig of a boy exactly as you do to your professional equals, listen to him with interest, and on occasions even feel you may have something to learn from him.'

Kafka's closest colleague did not conceal his dislike of Kafka and his personal visitors. As he wished to keep his distance from them, he always left the room, at least whenever I visited the office. Kafka then usually gave an unmistakable sigh of relief. He smiled, but it did not conceal the truth from me. So one day I said: 'Life with such a colleague must be difficult.'

Kafka raised his hand in sharp dissent.

'No, no! You're wrong. He is no worse than the rest of the staff. On the contrary; he's much better. He has a great deal of knowledge.'

I disagreed. 'Perhaps he only uses it to show off.'

Kafka nodded. 'Yes, that's possible. Many people do that, without doing any real work. But Treml really works hard.'

I sighed. 'Very well, you praise him, but all the same, you don't like him. You want your praise to conceal your dislike.'

Kafka's eyes flickered, he sucked his bottom lip in, while I continued with my analysis: 'To you, he's something alien. You look at him as if he were some strange beast in a cage.'

But at this Kafka looked me almost angrily in the eye, and said softly, in a voice taut with restrained feeling: 'You're mistaken. It's not Treml, but I, who am in the cage.'

'That's understandable. The office – '

Kafka interrupted me: 'Not only in the office, but every-where.' He laid his clenched fist on his chest. 'I carry the bars within me all the time.'

For a few seconds we looked at each other straight in the eye. Then came a knock at the door. My father entered. The tension vanished. We only talked about trivialities, but the sound of Kafka's words, 'I carry the bars within me,' re-echoed in my ears. Not only that day, but for many weeks and months. It was a glowing ember beneath the ashes of trivial incidents, but much later – I think in the spring or summer of 1922 – it suddenly leaped up like a fiercely burning flame.

*

In those days, I often used to meet a student called Bachrach who, so far as I knew, was only interested in three subjects: music, the English language and mathematics. He once said to me: 'Music is the sound of the soul, the direct voice of the subjective world. The English language mirrors a worldwide empire of finance. Mathematics plays a part in this. But that isn't important. Mathematics transcends the empire of crude accountancy. It is the root of every rational order, reaching out to the metaphysical.'

I always listened to his pronouncements in speechless astonishment. This pleased him. In return, he often gave me magazines, books and theatre tickets. So I was not surprised when he handed me a brand-new book.

'Today I have something very special for you.'

It was an English book, with the title, *Lady into Fox*, by David Garnett.4

'What good is it to me?' I said bitterly. 'You know perfectly well I don't read English.'

'Yes, I know. The book isn't meant for you to read. The book is only a proof of what I'm about to say. Your admired Kafka is becoming world-famous. This is demonstrated by the fact that he is being imitated. This book of Garnett's is a copy of *The Metamorphosis*.'

'A plagiarism?' I said sharply.

'No, I didn't say that. Garnett's book just has the same starting point. A lady changes into a vixen. A human being is transformed into an animal.'

'Could you lend me the book?'

'Of course. That's why I brought it. You can show it to Kafka.'

The next day I went to Franz Kafka's house, as he was not at his office. This was, incidentally, the first and last time I ever visited Franz Kafka at home. A thin lady dressed in black opened the door. Her beautiful grey-blue eyes, the shape of her mouth, and the slight arch of her nose showed that she was Kafka's mother.

I introduced myself as the son of one of Kafka's business colleagues and asked if I might speak to him.

'He is in bed. I'll ask,' she said.

She left me at the foot of the stairs. After a few minutes she returned. Her face shone with a kind of joy, which did not need to be put into words.

'He's pleased you've come. He's even asked for something to eat. But please don't stay for long. He's tired. He can't sleep.'

I promised to leave at once. Then I was taken through a long narrow ante-room, and a large room with dark brown furnishings into a smaller room where Kafka lay in a simple bed covered by a thin white counterpane.

He smiled, held his hand out to me, and with a tired gesture pointed to a chair at the foot of the bed. 'Please sit down. I shall probably not be able to talk for long. Please forgive me.'

'You must forgive me,' I said, 'for taking you by surprise. But I felt I had something really important to show you.'

I took the English book out of my pocket, laid it on the counterpane in front of Kafka, and told him about my latest conversation with Bachrach. When I said that Garnett's book imitated the method of *The Metamorphosis*, he gave a tired smile, and with a faint dissenting movement of his head said: 'But no! He didn't get that from me. It's a matter of the age. We both copied from that. Animals are closer to us than human beings. That's where our prison bars lie. We find relations with animals easier than with men.'

Kafka's mother came in.

'Can I bring you something?'

I stood up. 'No, thank you. I won't disturb you any longer.'

Frau Kafka looked at her son. He had lifted his chin and lay back with his eyes closed.

I said: 'I only wanted to bring the book.'

Franz Kafka opened his eyes and with a glance at the counterpane said: 'I will read it. Perhaps next week I'll be back at the office. I'll bring it with me.'

The following week he was not at the office. It was ten days or a fortnight before I was able to walk home with him. He gave me the book and said: 'Every man lives behind bars, which he carries within him. That is why people write so much about animals now. It's an expression of longing for a free natural life. But for human beings the natural life is a human life. But men don't always realize that. They refuse to realize it. Human existence is a burden to them, so they dispose of it in fantasies.'

I pursued his idea a step further: 'It's like the movement preceding the French Revolution, when people cried: Back to Nature!'

'Yes!' Kafka agreed. 'Only today people go further. They not only say it; they do it. Safe in the shelter of the herd, they march through the streets of the cities, to their work, to their feeding troughs, to their pleasures. It's like the narrowly confined life of the office. There are no longer any marvels, only regulations, prescriptions, directives. Men are afraid of freedom and responsibility. So they prefer to hide behind the prison bars which they build around themselves.'

*

About three weeks after my first meeting with Franz Kafka, I went for my first walk with him.

In the office he told me to wait for him at four o'clock at the Hus Memorial on the Altstädter Ring, and he would return to me an exercise-book of poems which I had lent him.

1 was at the appointed place at the appointed time, but Franz Kafka was nearly an hour late.

He apologized, 'I can never keep an appointment punctually. I am always too late. I am determined to be on time, I have the good and upright intention of keeping the appointment as agreed, but circumstances or my body always destroy this intention, in order to prove to me my own weakness. Probably that is the root of my illness.'

We walked along the Altstädter Ring.

Kafka said that it might be possible to publish some of my poems. He wished to give them to Otto Pick.5

'I have already discussed them with him,' he said.

I begged him not to publish the poems.

Kafka stood still.

'So you do not write in order to publish?'

'No. My poems are only an attempt, a very modest attempt, to prove to myself that I am not altogether stupid.'

We continued our walk. Franz Kafka showed me his parents' warehouse and house.

'So you are rich,' I said.

Franz Kafka pursed his mouth.

'What are riches? For someone an old shirt is riches. Others are poor on ten millions. Wealth is something completely relative and unsatisfying. Fundamentally, it is only a special situation. Wealth implies dependence on things which one possesses and which have to be safeguarded from dwindling away by new possessions and a further dependence. It is merely materialized insecurity. But – all that belongs to my parents, not me.'

My first walk with Franz Kafka ended in the following way:

Our circuit of the Ring had brought us back to the Kinsky Palace, when from out of the warehouse, with the business sign HERMANN KAFKA, emerged a tall, broad man in a dark overcoat and a shining hat. He remained standing about five steps away from us and waited.

As we came three paces nearer, the man said, very loudly:

'Franz. Go home. The air is damp.'

Kafka said, in a strangely gentle voice:

'My father. He is anxious about me. Love often wears the face of violence. Come and see me.'

I bowed. Franz Kafka departed, without shaking hands.[6]

*

A few days later I met Kafka by arrangement at five o'clock in the evening outside his father's warehouse. We intended to take a walk on the Hradschin. But Kafka was not well. He breathed with difficulty. So we merely strolled across the Altstädter Ring, past the Niklas Church in the Karpfengasse and by way of the Rathaus to the Kleine Ring. We stopped outside Calve's bookshop and looked into the windows.

I bent my head to right and left, trying to read the titles on the backs of the books. Kafka was amused, and laughed.

'So you too are a lunatic about books, with a head that wags from too much reading?'

'That's right. I don't think I could exist without books. To me, they're the whole world.'

Kafka's eyebrows narrowed.

'That's a mistake. A book cannot take the place of the world. That is impossible. In life, everything has its own meaning and its own purpose, for which there cannot be any permanent substitute. A man can't, for instance, master his own experience through the medium of another personality. That is how the world is in relation to books. One tries to imprison life in a book, like a songbird in a cage, but it's no good. On the contrary! Out of the abstractions one finds in books, one can only construct systems that are cages for oneself. Philosophers are only brightly clad Papagenos with their own different cages.'

He laughed. This was followed by a hollow, ugly cough. When the attack was over, he said with a smile: 'I have told the truth. You have just heard it and seen it. What other people do through the nose, I have to say with my lungs.' This gave me an unpleasant feeling. To repress it, I said: 'Have you caught cold? Haven't you got a temperature?'

Kafka gave a tired smile: 'No . . . I'm never warm enough. So I am always burning . . . from cold.'

He wiped the sweat from his forehead with his handkerchief. His tight-pressed lips were framed by two deeply cut lines at the corners of his mouth.

He held out his hand.

'Goodbye.'

I could find nothing to say.

*

I had called on Franz Kafka in his office at the very moment when a proof copy of his story, *In the Penal Settlement*, arrived by post. Kafka opened the grey wrapper, without knowing what it contained. But when he opened the green-and-black bound volume and recognized his work, he was obviously embarrassed.

He opened the drawer of his desk, looked at me, closed the drawer, and handed me the book.

'You will certainly want to see the book.'

I answered with a smile, opened the volume, gave a hurried look at the printing and paper and gave him the book back, as I realized his nervousness.

'It is beautifully done,' I said. 'A really representative Drugulin Press production. You should be very satisfied, Herr Doktor.'

'That I really am not,' said Franz Kafka, and pushed the book carelessly into a drawer, which he closed. 'Publication of some scribble of mine always upsets me.'

'Then why do you allow it to be printed?'

'That's just it! Max Brod, Felix Weltsch,7 all my friends always take possession of something I have written and then take me by surprise with a completed contract with the publisher. I do not want to cause them any unpleasantness, and so it all ends in the publication of things which are entirely personal notes or diversions. Personal proofs of my human weakness are printed, and even sold, because my friends, with Max Brod at their head, have conceived the idea of making literature out of them, and because I have not the strength to destroy this evidence of solitude.'

After a short pause he said in a different voice:

'What I have just said is, of course, an exaggeration, and a piece of malice against my friends. In fact, I am so corrupt and shameless that I myself co-operate in publishing these things. As an excuse for my own weakness, I make circumstances stronger than they really are. That, of course, is a piece of deceit. But after all, I am a lawyer. So I can never get away from evil.'

*

Kafka sat at his desk; tired, grey-faced, his arms hanging limply, his head bent slightly to one side. I could see that he was not well. I wanted to apologize and leave but he restrained me.

'Do stay. I'm glad you came. Tell me a story.'

I realized that he wanted to escape from his depression. So I let myself go, and told him a series of little anecdotes which I had heard or had been concerned in myself. I described some of the characters in the streets of the suburb where I lived with my parents, brawny innkeepers, house porters, some of my school friends, and told him about the old Karinthaler quay on the Moldau and the fierce battles that took place between the various street gangs, who usually employed the horse-dung lying about as a fearsome weapon of bombardment.

'Brr!' Kafka shivered. He was obsessively clean, and in the office washed his hands every other minute. Now he made a grimace, in which disgust and amusement were combined, as in some gnomish mask. His depression had lifted. So I could begin to talk about exhibitions, concerts and the books I spent nearly all day reading. Kafka was always amazed at the number of books I devoured.

'You're an absolute rubbish dump! What do you do at night? Do you sleep well?'

'I sleep deeply and soundly,' I said self-consciously. 'My conscience doesn't wake me up till morning. But then with such regularity that I might have a built-in alarm clock in my head.'

'And dreams – do you dream?'

I shrugged my shoulders. 'I don't know. Now and then after waking, I remember some fragment of a dream, but it's gone almost immediately. I hardly ever retain a dream in my memory. And even when I do it's usually something perfectly stupid and confused. Like the day before yesterday, for instance.'

'What did you dream?'

'I was in a huge store. I was walking with someone I didn't know through a large department, filled with bicycles, farm carts and locomotives. My companion said: "I'll never get a new cap now, which is what I wanted." I said frostily: "Why a new cap? You'd do better to buy yourself a nice, new face." – It should have made him angry, but he was quite unmoved – "You're quite right," he said. "We should get out of here into another department." – And indeed he at once hurried off to a flight of winding stairs. We immediately found ourselves in an enormous room, in a bluish-green light, where – as in some large ready-made clothing shop – various kinds of coats, jackets, ladies' costumes, men's suits were hanging on endless lines of racks, and inside them were different varieties of headless bodies, tall and short, fat and thin, with dangling arms and legs, so that overcome with fear I said to my companion: "These are all beheaded corpses!" – But my companion only laughed: "Nonsense. You know nothing about business. These aren't corpses." – At the same time he pointed to a rather dark passageway, where two bespectacled nurses were loading a stretcher on to a railway platform with the sign: *Tailoring – No Admittance*. The two nurses moved very circumspectly, taking very small steps, so that I had a good look at what they were carrying. It was a man who lay propped upon one elbow, like a reclining odalisque. He was wearing black patent leather shoes, striped trousers, and a dark grey frockcoat, such as my father usually wears on festive occasions.'

'Did the man on the stretcher remind you of your father?'

'No, I couldn't see his face at all. His head was hidden, right down to the opening of his waistcoat, by a great white muslin bandage, as if he were a badly wounded casualty. But all the same he seemed perfectly well. In one hand he had a slender black walking-stick with a curved silver handle which he twirled playfully in the air. With his other hand he held to the shapeless muslin ball of his head a shako which was perpetually slipping off: it was like the shako which my brother used to wear years ago on Sundays as a reservist in the Austrian artillery. I remembered this, and the memory made me lean forward into the passage to see who the man on the stretcher really was. Then suddenly the two nurses and the stretcher vanished, and I was standing in front of a little desk covered with ink spots, behind which sat your colleague Treml. Two men in long white linen coats suddenly appeared to right and left of me. I knew they were policemen disguised as hospital attendants and that under their linen coats they were wearing great holsters and scabbards for their pistols and sabres.'

Kafka sighed: 'Well! I suppose that frightened you.'

'Yes,' I said. 'I was afraid. Not so much of the two men, as of Treml, who gave me a cynical smile, and toyed with a slender, shining silver letter-opener as he spat out at me: "You have no right to your face. You are not the person you pretend to be. We'll peel your stolen skin from your face-bones." – Then he made a few vigorous strokes in the air with the letter-opener. I was frightened and looked round for my companion. Treml snarled: "Don't move! You can't escape!" – That made me furious. I screamed at him: "Who do you think you are, you jumped-up clerk? My father's above you in the office. I'm not afraid of your letter-opener." That struck home. Treml's face went green. He jumped up and shouted: "It's a surgical instrument! You'll soon see for yourself. Take him away!" – The two disguised policemen took hold of me. I wanted to scream. But the policeman's great black-haired hand was clapped over my mouth. I bit into his fist, which stank of sweat, and woke up. The blood was pulsing in my temples. I was drenched with sweat. It was the worst dream I have ever had.'

Kafka rubbed his chin with the back of his hand. 'I can believe that.' He bent over his desk and slowly knitted his fingers together. 'The world of the rag-trade is a hell, a stinking dung heap, a louse-hole.'

He looked at me for a few moments. I longed to know what he was about to say. Then he said in a perfectly normal, conversational voice: 'You're going to call on your father, aren't you? I still have work to do.' He smiled and held out his hand – 'Work is a release from the longings of our dreams, which often only blind us and flatter us to death.'

*

Franz Kafka was fascinated by the young. His story, *The Stoker*, is filled with tenderness and sympathy.[8] I told him this as we were discussing the Czech translation by Milena Jesenská, which had appeared in the literary review *Kmen* (*The Stem*).[9]

'There is so much sunshine and high spirits in your story. So much love – though it is never mentioned.'

'They are not in the story, but in the subject of the story – youth,' said Franz Kafka gravely. 'Youth is full of sunshine and love. Youth is happy, because it has the ability to see beauty. When this ability is lost, wretched old age begins, decay, unhappiness.'

'So age excludes the possibility of happiness?'

'No, happiness excludes age.' Smiling, he bent his head forward, as if to hide it between his hunched shoulders. 'Anyone who keeps the ability to see beauty never grows old.'

His smile, his attitude, his voice, reminded one of a quiet and serene boy.

'Then in *The Stoker* you are very young and happy.'

I had hardly finished the sentence than his expression darkened.

'*The Stoker* is very good,' I hastened to add, but Franz Kafka's dark grey eyes were filled with grief.

'One speaks best about what is strange to one. One sees it most clearly. *The Stoker* is the remembrance of a dream, of something that perhaps never really existed. Karl Rossmann is not a Jew. But we Jews are born old.'

*

On another occasion, when I told Kafka of a case of juvenile crime, we again discussed his story *The Stoker*.

I asked whether the character of the sixteen-year-old Karl Rossmann had been drawn from life.

Franz Kafka said, 'I had many models, and none. But all that is in the past.'

'The character of the young Rossmann, and that of the stoker, are so full of life,' I said.

Kafka's expression darkened.

'That is only a by-product. I was not describing people. I was telling a story. They are images, only images.'

'Then there must have been a model. The condition of an image is vision.'

Kafka smiled.

'One photographs things in order to get them out of one's mind. My stories are a kind of closing one's eyes.'

*

Conversations about his books were always very brief.

'I have been reading *The Verdict*.'

'Did you like it?'

'Like it? The book is horrifying!'

'You are perfectly right.'

'I should like to know how you came to write it. The dedication, *For F.*, is certainly not merely formal. Surely you wanted the book to say something to someone. I should like to know the context.'[10]

Kafka smiled, embarrassed.

'I am being impertinent. Forgive me.'

'You mustn't apologize. One reads in order to ask questions. *The Verdict* is the spectre of a night.'

'What do you mean?'

'It is a spectre,' he repeated, with a hard look into the distance.

'And yet you wrote it.'

'That is merely the verification, and so the complete exorcism, of the spectre.'

*

My friend Alfred Kämpf from Altsattel near Falkenau, whose acquaintance I had made in Elbogen, admired Kafka's story *The Metamorphosis*. He described the author as 'a new, more profound and therefore more significant Edgar Allan Poe'.

During a walk with Franz Kafka on the Altstädter Ring I told him about this new admirer of his, but aroused neither interest nor understanding. On the contrary, Kafka's expression showed that any discussion of his book was distasteful to him. I, however, was filled with a zeal for discoveries, and so I was tactless.

'The hero of the story is called Samsa,' I said. 'It sounds like a cryptogram for Kafka. Five letters in each word. The S in the word Samsa has the same position as the K in the word Kafka. The A . . .'

Kafka interrupted me.

'It is not a cryptogram. Samsa is not merely Kafka, and nothing else. *The Metamorphosis* is not a confession, although it is – in a certain sense – an indiscretion.'

'I know nothing about that.'

'Is it perhaps delicate and discreet to talk about the bugs in one's own family?'

'It isn't usual in good society.'

'You see what bad manners I have.'

Kafka smiled. He wished to dismiss the subject. But I did not wish to.

'It seems to me that the distinction between good and bad manners hardly applies here,' I said. '*The Metamorphosis* is a terrible dream, a terrible conception.'

Kafka stood still.

'The dream reveals the reality, which conception lags behind. That is the horror of life – the terror of art. But now I must go home.'

He took a curt farewell.

Had I driven him away?

I felt ashamed.

*

We did not see each other for a fortnight. I told him about the books which in the meanwhile I had 'devoured'. Kafka smiled.

'From life one can extract comparatively so many books, but from books so little, so very little, life.'

'So literature is a bad preservative?'

He laughed and nodded.

*

Franz Kafka and I often laughed long and loud together, that is to say, if one could ever describe Franz Kafka's laughter as loud. For me at least what has remained in my memory is not the sound of his laughter but the physical gestures by which he expressed his amusement. Depending on how much he was amused, he threw his head back quickly or slowly, opened his mouth a little and closed his eyes into narrow slits, as if his face were turned up to the sun. Or he laid his hand on the desk, raised his shoulders, drew in his bottom lip and shut his eyes as if someone were going to shower him with water.

In this kind of mood I once told him a little Chinese story I had read a short time before – I can't remember where.

'The heart is a house with two bedrooms. In one lives Suffering and in the other Joy. One mustn't laugh too loud, or one will wake the sorrow in the next-door room.'

'And Joy? Isn't she woken by the noise of sorrow?'

'No. Joy is hard of hearing. So she never hears the suffering in the next room.'

Kafka nodded. 'That's right. That's why one often only pretends to be enjoying oneself. One stuffs one's ears up with the wax of pleasure. For instance, me. I simulate gaiety, in order to vanish behind it. My laughter is a concrete wall.'

'Against whom?'

'Naturally, against myself.'

'But a wall is turned against the outer world,' I said. 'It's a defence against what comes from outside.'

But Kafka instantly and decisively repudiated such a view.

'Is it, indeed? Every defence is a retreat, a withdrawal. A blow at the world is always a blow at oneself. For that reason, every concrete wall is only an illusion, which sooner or later crumbles away. For Inner and Outer belong to each other. Divided, they become two bewildering aspects of a mystery which we endure but can never solve.'

*

A rainy, damp October day. In the corridors of the Accident Insurance Institution the lights were on. Kafka's office was like a twilit cave. He sat bent low over his desk. In front of him lay an octavo sheet of greyish office paper. In his hand was a long yellow pencil. As I approached him, he laid the pencil down on the paper, which was covered with hastily executed sketches of strange figures.

'You've been drawing?'

Kafka gave an apologetic smile: 'No! These are only doodles.'

'May I look? As you know, I'm very interested in drawing.'

'But these aren't drawings to be shown to anyone. They are purely personal, and therefore illegible, hieroglyphs.'

He took the piece of paper and with both hands pressed it into a ball which he tossed into a waste-paper basket beside the desk. 'My figures have no proper spatial proportions. They have no horizon of their own. The perspective of the shapes I try to capture lies outside the paper, at the other unsharpened end of the pencil – in myself!'

He reached into the waste-paper basket, took out the ball of paper he had just thrown in, smoothed out the crumpled sheets and tore it into very small pieces, which with a vigorous gesture he swept into the basket again.

I surprised Kafka drawing on several occasions and each time he threw his 'doodles', as he called his drawings, crumpled up into the waste-paper basket or hid them quickly in the middle drawer of his desk. One would guess that his drawings were an even more intimate and private matter than his writing. This naturally inspired me with a growing curiosity, which I exerted myself to hide from Kafka. I behaved as if I never noticed the hasty sweeping away of the drawings. Yet my pretence always left a sense of strain and constraint behind. I could not talk and listen as easily and without embarrassment as before, when nothing – or so I believed – had been concealed from me.

This did not escape Kafka's notice, he realized my uneasiness, and so one day, when I had once more caught him drawing, he pushed his writing pad over to me and, avoiding my eyes, said: 'Take a look at my doodles. There's no sense in my continuing to arouse an unsatisfied curiosity about them, which I force you to disguise. Please don't be annoyed with me.'

There was nothing I could say. I felt as if I had been caught out in an act of indecency. At first, I felt that I should simply push the drawings back across the table. Then I pulled myself together and with my head bent sharply to one side looked obliquely at the paper. It was covered with strange minute sketches, in which only the abstraction of movement was emphasized, of tiny men running, fighting and crawling, and kneeling on the ground.

I was disappointed.

'But these aren't anything. You really didn't need to hide them from me. They're perfectly harmless sketches.'

Kafka slowly wagged his head to and fro – 'Oh no! They are not as harmless as they look. These drawings are the remains of an old, deep-rooted passion. That's why I tried to hide them from you.'

I looked again at the paper and its little men.

'But I don't understand you, Herr Doctor. What passion is there here?'

Kafka smiled indulgently. – 'Naturally it's not on the paper. The passion is in me. I always wanted to be able to draw. I wanted to see, and to hold fast to what was seen. That was my passion.'

'Did you take drawing lessons?'

'No. I tried to define what I saw in a way that was my own. My drawings are not pictures, but private ideograms.' Kafka smiled. – 'I am still in Egyptian bondage. I have not yet crossed the Red Sea.'

I laughed: 'The first thing after the Red Sea is the desert.'

Kafka nodded: 'Yes, in the Bible and everywhere else.'

He pushed his hands against the edge of the desk, leaned back in his chair, and, his body relaxed, stared up at the ceiling.

'The false illusion of a freedom achieved by external means is an error, a confusion, a desert in which nothing flourishes except the two herbs of fear and despair. That is inevitable, because anything which has a real and lasting value is always a gift from within. Man doesn't grow from below upwards but from within outwards. That is the fundamental condition of all freedom in life. It is not an artificially constructed social environment but an attitude to oneself and to the world which it is a perpetual struggle to maintain. It's the condition of man's freedom.'

'The condition?' I asked doubtfully.

'Yes,' said Kafka, and repeated his definition.

'But that is a complete paradox!' I cried.

Kafka took a deep breath. Then he said: 'Yes, in fact it is. The spark which constitutes our conscious life must bridge the gap of the contradiction and leap from one pole to the other, so that for one moment we can see the world as if revealed in a flash of lightning.'

I was silent for a moment. Then I pointed to the paper with its drawings and asked quietly: 'And the little men – what about them?'

'They come out of the dark to vanish into the dark,' said Kafka, pulled out a drawer, swept the scribble-covered paper into it, and said, in a completely unemotional voice: 'My drawing is a perpetually renewed and unsuccessful attempt at primitive magic.'

I stared at him uncomprehendingly, and must have looked very stupid. The corners of Kafka's mouth twitched. He was obviously suppressing a smile. He hid his mouth behind his raised hand, coughed and said: 'Everything in the human world is a picture that has come to life. When the Eskimos want to set fire to a piece of wood, they draw a few wavy lines on it. That is the magical picture of fire, which they'll bring to life by rubbing their fire-sticks together. That's what I do. Through my drawings I want to come to terms with the shapes which I perceive. But my figures don't take fire. Perhaps I don't use the right material. Perhaps my pencil doesn't have the right powers. It's also possible that it's only myself, and nothing else, that lacks the necessary powers.'

'That must be so,' I agreed, and at the same time tried to

smile ironically. 'After all, Doctor Kafka, you're no Eskimo.'

'Quite right. I'm no Eskimo, but like most people today I live in a bitterly cold world. But we neither have the furs of the Eskimos, nor their other means of existence. Compared with them, we're stark naked.' He pursed his lips. – 'Today the warmest clad are the wolves in sheep's clothing; they manage very well. They're properly dressed. What do you think?'

I disagreed. 'Thank you, no. I'd rather freeze.'

'Me too!' cried Kafka, and pointed to the central heating radiator, on which water was steaming in an oblong tin dish. 'We don't want our own or borrowed furs. We'd rather stick to our comfortable desert of ice.' We both laughed: Kafka to cover up my incomprehension, and I – to accept his kindness as something that goes without saying.

*

I was very distressed when I called on Kafka.

'What is the matter? Your face is quite grey.'

'That will soon be over,' I managed to say, and tried to smile. 'People think I'm something that I'm not.'

'That's not unusual,' declared Kafka, with a slightly contemptuous curl of the lip. 'It's an old failing of human communication. The only thing that's always new about it is the pain it causes.' – He took a document from his desk. 'Stay and sit here quietly for a moment. I've something I must do in the meanwhile. I'll come back immediately. Shall I lock the door for a moment so that you shan't be disturbed?'

'No, thank you. I'll soon feel better.'

Kafka quietly left the room. I leaned back in the chair.

At that time I suffered, at quite irregular and therefore unpredictable intervals, from intense headaches, which were caused by an exaggerated sensibility of the facial nerves – trigeminus. Nearly an hour previously, I had suffered such an attack on my way to the Workmen's Accident Insurance Institution. I had to lean against a hoarding on the Florenz near the Staatsbahnhof and wait patiently until the attack had passed. The climax came with a violent attack of sweating together with a kind of convulsive seizure. But this was also the point from which the attack swiftly subsided. I got better from minute to minute, but remained quietly beside the hoarding, as my legs were trembling under me.

People gave me unpleasant and, so it seemed to me, contemptuous looks as they passed by. Then an elderly woman said to her younger companion: 'Just look at that! Hardly out of short trousers but blind drunk already! What a wretch! What on earth will become of him.'

I wanted to explain my condition to the woman but couldn't utter a word. Before I could pull myself together, the two of them had disappeared round the next corner. So I walked slowly to the Accident Insurance Institution. I was still weak in the knees, but Kafka's voice was like a stimulating tonic to me, and there was the quiet which calmed my agitation, and in a few moments the last traces of the attack had disappeared.

When Kafka returned, I told him what had happened to me on the Florenz, and ended my story with the words: 'I ought to have shut the woman up and returned her insults! Instead, I didn't say a word. What a wretched coward I am!'

But Kafka shook his head. 'Don't say that! You don't realize how much strength there is in silence. Aggression is usually only a disguise which conceals one's weakness from oneself and from the world. Genuine and lasting strength consists in bearing things. Only weaklings react quickly and brutally. And in doing so, they sacrifice their manhood.'

Kafka opened the drawer of his desk and took out a magazine. It was No. 21 in the fourth yearly issue of the journal *Kmen* (German: *Der Stamm* – The Stem) which he placed in front of me.

He said to me: 'On the first page there are four poems. One is very touching. It's called *Pokora* – Humility.' I read:

> *I'll grow smaller and smaller*
> *Till I'm the smallest thing on earth.*
> *On an early morning, in a summer meadow*

I'll stretch my hand to the smallest flower
And hide my face in it, whispering:
On you, little child, without shoes or clothes,
Heaven leans its hand
In a flashing drop of dew
So that its giant sky
Shan't break in pieces.[11]

I said quietly: 'That is poetry.'

'Yes,' answered Kafka, 'that is poetry – Truth clothed in the language of friendship and love. Everything, the prickliest thistle just as much as the most elegant palm tree supports the heavenly firmament above us, so that the giant sky, the giant sky of our world, shan't break in pieces. Forget about your meeting in the street today. The woman made a mistake. Probably she can't tell the difference between the appearance and the reality. That's a crime. She is a poor woman. Her sense of feeling is warped. How often she must have bruised herself against even the smallest things.' He gently touched my hand, which lay on the magazine in front of me like a paperweight and said with a smile, 'The road from appearance to reality is often very hard and long, and many people make only very poor travellers. We must forgive them when they stagger against us as if against a brick wall.'

*

I received a rude letter filled with abuse from an acquaintance to whom I had lent small sums of money and now couldn't afford to lend any more. Conceited ape, ox and idiot were among its mildest expressions.

I showed it to Kafka, who laid it on the edge of his desk with the tips of his fingers, as if it were some dangerous object. Then he said:

'Swearing is something horrible. This letter seems to me like some smoking fire which burns one's lungs and eyes. Swearing destroys man's greatest invention – language. It is an insult to the soul and a murderous offence against grace. But so is any use of words without proper consideration. For to speak implies to consider and define. Words involve a decision between life and death.'

'Do you think I should get a lawyer's letter written to the fellow?' I asked.

Kafka shook his head vigorously.

'No! To what purpose? In any case, he wouldn't take such a warning seriously. And even if he would – leave him alone. Sooner or later the ox he talks of will toss him on his horns. Men can never avoid the ghosts they have called into the world. Evil always returns to its point of origin.'

*

I surprised Franz Kafka in his office studying a catalogue of the *Reclam-Bücherei*.

'I am getting drunk on book titles,' said Kafka. 'Books are a narcotic.'

I opened my brief-case and showed him the contents.

'I am a hashish addict, Herr Doktor.'

Kafka was amazed.

'Nothing but new books!'

I emptied the brief-case on to his writing-desk. Kafka took one book after the other, turned the pages, read a passage here and there, and returned me the book.

'And you are going to read all that?'

I nodded.

Kafka pursed his lips.

'You spend too much time on ephemeras. The majority of modern books are merely wavering reflections of the present. They disappear very quickly. You should read more old books. The classics. Goethe. What is old reveals its deepest value – lastingness. What is merely new is the most transitory of all things. It is beautiful today, and tomorrow merely ludicrous. That is the way of literature.'

'And poetry?'

'Poetry transforms life. Sometimes that is even worse.'

A knock at the door. Enter my father.

'Is my son and heir being a nuisance?'

Kafka smiled.

'Oh, no! We are discussing devils and demons.'

*

When I think of it today, I have to confess that I was quite ruthless in my conduct to Kafka; I often called at his office without warning and just as and when it suited me. Yet he always greeted me with a friendly smile and a hand stretched out in welcome. It's true that I always asked, 'Am I disturbing you?' But Kafka always answered with a negative shake of the head or a negligently dismissive wave of the hand.

Once he explained:

'To be disturbed by an unexpected visit is a weakness, an avoidance of the unexpected. One huddles into one's so-called private life, because one lacks the strength to master the world. One flies from the miraculous into one's own limited self. That is a withdrawal. Being is most of all a being-with-things, a dialogue. One mustn't shrink from that. You can always call on me as and when you please.'

*

Kafka noticed that I was short of sleep. I told him truthfully that 'I had been so full of things that I had written throughout the night'. Kafka placed his large hands, that looked as if carved out of wood, on top of the desk and said: 'It's a great good fortune to be able to direct one's inner feeling so directly into the open.'

'It was an intoxication. I haven't yet read what I've written.'

'Naturally. What one writes is only the ashes of one's experience.'

*

My friend Ernst Lederer wrote poems in especially bright blue ink on engraved sheets of hand-made paper.[12]

I told Kafka about it.

He said, 'That is quite right. Every magician has his own

rites. Haydn for example only composed in a ceremonially powdered wig. Writing is, after all, a kind of invocation of spirits.'

*

Alfred Kämpf gave me the three volumes of Edgar Allan Poe's *Selected Tales*, in an omnibus edition published by the *Reclam-Verlag*. I showed Kafka the little book, which I carried about with me continually for several weeks. He turned the pages, read some of their contents, and then asked me: 'Do you know about Poe's life?'

'I only know what I've been told by Kämpf. It seems that Poe was a notorious drunkard.'

Kafka frowned.

'Poe was ill. He was a poor devil who had no defences against the world. So he fled into drunkenness. Imagination only served him as a crutch. He wrote tales of mystery to make himself at home in the world. That's perfectly natural. Imagination has fewer pitfalls than reality does.'

'You've made a close study of Poe?'

'No. In fact I know very little about his writings. But I know his way of escape, and his dreamer's face. They are always the same. One can see them again for instance in this book.'

Kafka opened the middle drawer of his desk and handed me a greenish-blue linen-bound book: *Treasure Island*, by Robert Louis Stevenson. 'Stevenson was tubercular,' said Kafka, while I hastily turned the title page of the book and looked inside. 'So he emigrated to the South Seas. He lived there on an island. But he saw nothing of it. For him, the world he lived in was simply the stage for a child's dream about pirates, a spring-board for the imagination.'

'So far as I can see at first glance,' I said, nodding at the book, which I had put down on the desk, 'he also describes the sea and the men and the tropical vegetation of the South Pacific.'

'Yes, and indeed he does it very thoroughly.'

'So his book is also a piece of reality?'

'Of course,' said Kafka. 'Dreams always directly embody a mass of one's day-to-day experiences.'

'Perhaps,' I said cautiously, 'in one's dreams one's trying to come to terms with one's guilt in regard to one's experience. Do you think that's true?'

'Yes, that's right,' said Kafka. 'Reality is always the strongest force shaping the world and human beings. It really changes things. That is why it has reality. One can't escape it. Dreams are only a way round, at the end of which one always returns to the world of most immediate reality. Stevenson to his treasure island and I – .' He broke off.

'And you – – '; I continued where he left off, 'to your office here and your home in the Altstädter Ring.'

'You're quite right,' sighed Kafka.

Suddenly his face had an expression so ravaged by care that I could not help mumbling an apology: 'Please forgive my impertinence, Herr Doktor. I talk too much. That's my weakness.'

'On the contrary,' said Kafka. 'It's a form of strength. Your impressions take shape in words more quickly than other people's. There's nothing to forgive.'

I shook my head. 'Yes, there is. I've behaved badly.'

Kafka raised his left arm to shoulder height, let it fall limply, and then said with an enchanting smile: 'That's also quite in order. You do behave badly. As yet you don't belong to the world of petrified good manners. So your words are still – to return to Stevenson's South Sea island – a sharp, unblunted bushman's knife. You must take care not to hack away with it so that you mutilate yourself. Next to murder, that's the worst of crimes against life.'

*

Among the boys I met in summer in the swimming baths and in winter at the skating rink was a certain Leo Weisskopf, a slim, bespectacled, wavy-haired blond youth with a round, rosy, girl's face. His father had an office on the Peterplatz, where he conducted a wholesale business in chemical products.

This made Leo Weisskopf a member of the 'upper bourgeoisie'. He was always very polite, with ingratiating manners, but was without any kind of affectation. His clothes matched his behaviour. In conversation he was very reserved but extremely agreeable. But though no one could ever have called him a spoil-sport or a wet blanket, one could never feel really at ease in his company. His presence threw a damper on everything. My friend Ernst Lederer therefore used to call Leo Weisskopf, who was slightly his junior, a sneak.

He said: 'He's friendly and agreeable, but only in order to elude us. He hides himself from us.'

'Why should he do that?'

My friend shrugged his shoulders. 'How should I know? I just feel it.'

'You don't like him,' I said. 'That's all it is.'

'You're right,' Ernst Lederer agreed. 'My dislike is entirely a matter of feeling. Leo Weisskopf is different from us. There's something obscure and intangible that divides him from us. Perhaps in some kind of way he is not quite normal. Perhaps he's addicted to some secret vice.'

To which I replied loftily: 'And perhaps you're an idiot.' But my friend, who was usually very touchy, only answered very quietly: 'Either you are or I am. Time will tell.'

That ended our discussion of Leo Weisskopf.

Two days later we heard – I don't remember how or from whom – that Leo Weisskopf was dead. Suicide. Cyanide. It was said that he was in love with a much older woman. Whether in fact this was his only reason for killing himself, we never knew. Ernst Lederer doubted it. I told Franz Kafka the story. He listened with his eyes closed. When I had finished my account, he was silent for one or two minutes, then said, looking at the ceiling: 'That's a very obscure incident. A man is only fully aware of himself when he's either in love or in danger of death. Perhaps your friend was disillusioned by the woman he loved. Perhaps she only used him as a passing plaything. Perhaps he thought his life was completely pointless without the woman he loved. Perhaps he wished to show her what he thought of her by his death. Perhaps he wanted to tell her that, after she had left him, all that remained to him was the right to dispose of himself as he wished. Do you understand?'

'Yes,' I said.

Kafka continued. 'One can only throw away what really belongs to one. So suicide can be regarded as a form of egotism raised to the point of absurdity. As a form of egotism, which usurps the right to commit violence against God, whereas in fact there can be no question of violence in such a case, because there is no strength. The suicide only kills himself out of impotence. Because he cannot do anything else. So he takes the last course left open to him. For this, he does not require any strength. All that's required is despair, the abandonment of all hope. No risk is involved. To dare is to endure, to give oneself to life, to carry on as if untroubled from one day to another.'

*

Franz Kafka asked me several times to show him some of my 'unrhymed scribbles' – as I myself described them. I therefore looked through my notebook for suitable extracts, which I put together as a collection of short prose pieces, gave it the title *The Moment of the Abyss*, and presented it to Kafka.

He only gave me back the manuscript after several months, when he was preparing to travel to the sanatorium at Tatranské Matlyary.

As he did so, he said:

'All your stories are so touchingly young. You say far more about the impressions which things inspire in you than about the things and objects themselves. That is lyrical poetry. You caress the world, instead of grasping it.'

'So my writing is worthless?'

Kafka grasped my hand.

'I did not say that. Certainly these little stories have a value for you. Every written word is a personal document. But art . . .'

'Art is different,' I continued bitterly.

'Your writing is not yet art,' said Kafka firmly. 'This description of feelings and impressions is most of all a hesitant groping for the world. The eyes are still heavy with dreams. But in time that will cease and then perhaps the outstretched groping hand will withdraw as if caught by the fire. Perhaps you will cry out, stammer incoherently, or grind your teeth together and open your eyes wide, very wide. But – these are only words. Art is always a matter of the entire personality. For that reason it is fundamentally tragic.'

*

I had made an appointment to meet Kafka at his office. On the previous day my father brought me a copy of the Berlin *Aktion*[13] and a message from Kafka that he would not be in the office until the following week. When finally we met, he greeted me and then said immediately: 'Could you read my writing?'

'Yes, very well. Your writing runs in a clearly flowing curve.'

Kafka folded his hands on his desk and said, with a bitter-sweet look: 'It's the curve of a rope falling to the ground. My letters are nooses.'

I wanted to relieve Kafka of the depression which his words revealed. So I smiled and said: 'Then they're lassos.'

Kafka silently nodded.

I went on teasing him: 'What do you hope to catch with your lassos?' With a faint shrug of his shoulders, Kafka answered: 'I don't know. Perhaps I'm trying to reach some unseen shore, which I've long ago been swept past by the rushing stream of my weakness.'

Franz Kafka showed me a questionnaire of an inquiry into literature which I think Otto Pick had drawn up for the Sunday literary supplement of the *Prager Presse*.

He pointed with his forefinger to the question: *What can you say about your future literary plans?* and smiled: 'That's a silly question. It's impossible to answer.'

I looked at him without understanding.

'Can one predict how one's heart will beat tomorrow? No,

it's not possible. The pen is only a seismographic pencil for the heart. It will register earthquakes, but can't predict them.'

*

I called on Doctor Kafka in his office. He was just about to go as I entered.

'You're going?'

'Only for a moment, two floors higher in your father's department. Sit down and wait for me. I shall not be long. In the meanwhile, perhaps, look at this new review. It came by post yesterday.'

It was the first number of a large, representative review appearing in Berlin. It was called *Marsyas*, and was edited by Theodore Tagger.[14] Inside was a prospectus, in which, among notices of promised contributions, a work of Franz Werfel's, *Theoretical Prose*, was announced. He was a friend of Kafka's, so on his return to the office I asked him whether he knew anything about the announcement.

'Yes,' said Franz Kafka curtly. 'Werfel told Max it was an invention of the publisher's.'

'Can one do such things? After all, that is a lie.'

'It is literature,' said Kafka smiling. 'Flight from reality.'

'So poetry is lies?'

'No. Poetry is a condensate, an essence. Literature, on the other hand, is a relaxation, a means of pleasure which alleviates the unconscious life, a narcotic.'

'And poetry?'

'Poetry is exactly the opposite. Poetry is an awakening.'

'So poetry tends towards religion.'

'I would not say that. But certainly to prayer.'

*

On another occasion, when Kafka and I were visiting the Franciscan church in the Jungmannplatz, we saw, immediately beside the entrance, under a dark altar piece, an old woman praying passionately. When we left the church he said to me:

'Prayer and art are passionate acts of will. One wants to

transcend and enhance the will's normal possibilities. Art like prayer is a hand outstretched in the darkness, seeking for some touch of grace which will transform it into a hand that bestows gifts. Prayer means casting oneself into the miraculous rainbow that stretches between becoming and dying, to be utterly consumed in it, in order to bring its infinite radiance to bed in the frail little cradle of one's own existence.'

*

I often marvelled at Kafka's wide knowledge of all the varied architectural features of the city. He was familiar not only with its palaces and churches but also with the most obscure alleys of the Old Town. He knew the medieval names of the houses even though their ancient signs no longer hung over their entrances but in the city museum in the Pŏríč. Kafka read the city's history out of the walls of its ancient houses. He conducted me by crooked alleyways into narrow, funnel-shaped interior courtyards in Old Prague, which he called 'spittoons of light'; he walked with me, near the old Charles Bridge, through a baroque entrance hall, across a court no bigger than a handkerchief with round Renaissance arches and through a dark tubular tunnel, to a tiny inn enclosed in a small court which bore the name of *The Stargazer* (Czech: *U hvezdáru*), because here Johannes Kepler had lived for many years, and here, in the year 1609, his famous book, which far outstripped all the scientific knowledge of his day, the *Astronomia Nova* was born.

Kafka loved the streets, palaces, gardens and churches of the city where he was born. He looked with joyful interest through the pages of all the books on the antiquities of Prague which I brought to him in his office. His eyes and hands literally caressed the pages of such publications, though he had read them all long before I placed them on his desk. His eyes shone with the look of a passionate collector. Yet he was the precise opposite of a collector. The past was for him not some historically dead collector's piece, but a supple instrument of knowledge. a bridge to today.

I realized this once when, on the way from the Accident Insurance Institution to the Altstädter Ring, Kafka and I came to a halt at the Jacobskirche, immediately opposite the Teinhof.

'Do you know this church?' Kafka asked me.

'Yes. But only superficially. I know it belongs to the Franciscan Minorites nearby but that's all.'

'But you must certainly have seen the hand that hangs from a chain in the church.'

'Yes, several times even.'

'Shall we go and look at the hand together?'

'I'd like to very much.'

We entered the church, whose three naves enclose one of the largest ecclesiastical areas in Prague. On the left, immediately beside the entrance, there hung from a long iron chain fixed to the roof a smoke-blackened bone, covered with shreds of dried flesh and sinew, which by its appearance might have been the pathetic remains of a human forearm. It was said to have been hacked off a thief in the year 1400, or soon after the Thirty Years War, and to have been hung in the church 'in eternal memory' of the incident.

According to the chronicles, and to a perpetually renewed verbal tradition, the story of this cruel deed was as follows: On one of the subsidiary altars in the church, which even today is still adorned by many side chapels, there stood a carved wooden statue of the Virgin, hung with gold and silver chains. Attracted by such wealth, a demobilized mercenary hid himself in a confessional where he waited for the church to close. Then he left his hiding place, approached the altar, stood on a stool which the verger normally used when lighting the altar candles, stretched out his hand and tried to take hold of the statue's adornments. But his hand was paralysed. The thief, who had never entered a church before, thought that his hand was being firmly held by the statue. He tried to free himself, but in vain. In the morning he was discovered lying senseless across the stool by the verger, who alarmed the monks. Soon a large crowd of people collected in prayer around the altar, where the statue of the Mother of God still held fast to the terrified figure of the thief; among them were the Burgomeister and some of the most prominent citizens of the old town. The verger and the monks tried to remove the thief's hand from the statue, but could not. The Burgomeister therefore summoned the hangman, who with one stroke of his sword severed the thief's forearm from his body. Then 'the statue likewise released the hand of the thief'. The forearm fell to the ground. The thief was bound up and a few days later he was sentenced to a long term of imprisonment for attempting to rob the church; when he had served his sentence he entered the Minorite order as a lay brother. The severed hand was attached to an iron chain in the church near the tombstone of the Prague city councillor Scholle von Schollenbach. On the pillar nearby was hung a primitive pictorial rendering of the event with an explanatory text in Latin, German and Czech.

Kafka looked hard at the withered remains of the arm for a moment, threw a glance at the text describing the miracle, and left the church. I followed him.

'How dreadful,' I said. 'Of course, the miracle of the Madonna was merely the effect of cramp.'

'But what caused it?' said Kafka.

I said: 'Probably some sudden sense of fear. The religious feeling that lay concealed under the thief's greed for the Virgin's treasures was suddenly released by his action. It was stronger than the thief realized. So his hand became paralysed.'

'Precisely!' said Franz Kafka, and put his hand under my arm. 'The longing for the divine, the sense of shame at the violation of holiness which always accompanies it, men's innate demand for justice – these are mighty and invincible forces, which grow stronger as men try to oppose them. They exert a moral control. A criminal must therefore suppress these forces in himself before he can commit an objectively criminal act. For that reason, every crime is preceded by a spiritual mutilation. In the mercenary who wanted to rob the statue this failed to occur. Therefore his hand became paralysed. It was crippled by his own need of justice. So to him the executioner's swordstroke was less dreadful than you imagine. On the contrary; the shock and the pain brought him salvation. The executioner's physical act took the place of spiritual mutilation. It liberated the wretched, unemployed mercenary, who could not even rob a wooden doll, from the cramp of conscience. He could continue to live as a human being.' We walked on in silence. Halfway along the little street which ran from the Teinhof to the Altstädter Ring, Kafka suddenly halted and asked: 'What are you thinking of?'

'I was wondering whether something like the story of the thief in the Jacobskirche was still possible today,' I answered eagerly and looked questioningly at Franz Kafka. But he only drew his eyebrows together. After a few steps he said: 'I think – hardly. Today the longing for God and the fear of sin are gravely enfeebled. We have sunk into a morass of presumption. This was shown by the war, in which for years men's moral strength, and themselves with it, was anaesthetized by mere dehumanization. I believe that today the violator of a church would no longer be struck by paralysis. And if such a thing happened, men would not hack away the thief's arm; they would amputate his antiquated moral imagination. They would send him to a lunatic asylum. There they would simply analyse out of existence the archaic moral impulses which had revealed themselves in hysterical paralysis.'

I grinned. 'The robber of churches would be transformed into the victim of a suppressed Oedipus, or mother, complex. After all, he wanted to rob the Mother of God.'

'Of course,' Kafka agreed. 'Today there is no sin and no longing for God. Everything is completely mundane and utilitarian. God lies outside our existence. And therefore all of us suffer a universal paralysis of conscience. All transcendental conflicts appear to have vanished, and yet all of them defend themselves like the wooden figure in the Jacobskirche. We are immobilized. We are completely transfixed. More than that! Most of us are simply glued to the shaky stool of vulgar common sense by the filth of fear. That is our entire way of life. I – for instance, sit in my office in the Accident Insurance Institution, look at documents and try to conceal my distaste for the whole Institution behind an expression of solemnity. Then you appear. We talk about everything under the sun, walk through the noisy streets into the quiet of the Jacobskirche, look at the severed hand and discuss the moral paralysis of our times and I go into my parents' shop for something to eat and write a few polite warning letters to some outstanding debtors. But nothing happens. The world is in order. Only we are transfixed like the wooden figure in the church. But without an altar.' He touched me lightly on the shoulder – 'Goodbye.'

*

Kafka and I were walking through the Zeltnergasse to the Altstädter Ring. From afar off we could hear the noise and singing of some large crowd; then, at *The White Peacock* inn we were pressed against the walls by a slowly marching column of demonstrators.

'There you see the strength of the International,' I said with a laugh, but Kafka's face darkened.

'Are you deaf? Can't you hear what these people are singing? They're singing brazenly nationalist songs from the old Austria.'

I protested: 'Then why the red flag?'

'That's nothing! Just a new dress for old passions,' Franz Kafka said, took me by the hand and led me across a dark courtyard in the house behind us, along a short passage and some white-washed steps into the narrow Gemsegasse and from there through the Eisengasse until we emerged in the broad Rittergasse, where nothing could be heard of the demonstration.

'I can't bear these street disturbances,' said Kafka with a sigh. 'They have in them the terror of godless wars of religion which begin with flags, songs and music and end in pillage and blood.'

I protested: 'That's not true! There are demonstrations almost every day in Prague now and they all end peaceably. The only blood that's spilt is in their black puddings.'

'That's only because things go slowly here. But that makes no difference. Such things will soon happen.'

Kafka waved his hands a couple of times, to show his concern, and continued: 'We live in an evil time, that is clear from the fact that nothing is called by its right name any more. We use the word *Internationalism* and by it we mean Humanity, that is to say, an ethical value, whereas in fact Internationalism is in practice primarily a geographical expression. It's as if ideas had lost their kernel and were simply manipulated like empty nutshells. So for instance we talk today about our homeland, at the very moment when men's roots have been ripped out of the ground long ago.'

'Who is to blame?' I said.

'We are all to blame. We all take part in such uprooting.'

'Yet there must be some force behind it?' I said obstinately. 'Who is it? Who are you thinking of?'

'No one! I'm not thinking of the driver or the driven. I simply see what is happening. Individuals are beside the point. And after all – how can a dramatic critic judge the performance of the actors when he's among them on the stage. He cannot detach himself. So everything becomes uncertain, loses balance. We live in a morass of corroding lies and illusions, in which terrible and monstrous things happen, which journalists report with amused objectivity and thus – without anyone noticing – trample on the lives of millions of people as if they were worthless insects.' I did not know how to reply.

We walked in silence through the Melantrichgasse and past the old Town Hall so as to reach Kafka's home on the corner of the Altstädter and the Pariser Strasse. Near the Hus Memorial, Kafka said: 'Everything sails under a false flag, no word corresponds to the truth. I, for instance – I am now going home. But it only looks as if I were. In reality, I mount into a prison specially constructed for myself, which is all the harsher because it looks like a perfectly ordinary bourgeois home and – except for myself – no one would recognize it as a prison. For that reason, every attempt at escape is useless. One cannot break one's chains when there are no chains to be seen. One's imprisonment is therefore organized as a perfectly ordinary, not over-comfortable form of daily life. Everything looks as if it were made of solid, lasting stuff. But on the contrary it is a life in which one is falling towards an abyss. It isn't visible. But if one closes one's eyes, one can hear its rush and roar.'

*

I showed Franz Kafka the outline of a drama on a biblical theme.

'What will you do with it?' he asked.

'I don't know. The material attracts me, but the treatment ... To complete the outline now seems to me a kind of scissors-and-paste work.'

Kafka gave me the manuscript.

'You are right. Only what is born lives. Everything else is a waste of time: literature with no justification to existence.'

*

I bought Kafka a Czech anthology of French religious poetry.[15] Kafka turned the pages of the little volume for a few moments. Then he carefully handed it me back across the desk.

'This kind of literature conveys a sophisticated kind of pleasure which I don't enjoy. Religion is continuously distilled into aesthetics. The power which gives meaning to life is transformed into a source of charm, a form of ostentatious display, like, for instance, expensive curtains, pictures, antique furniture and genuine Persian carpets. In such literature, religion becomes snobbery.'

'That's true,' I agreed. 'As a result of the war, substitutes were discovered even in the sphere of faith. This kind of literature is one of them. The poet wears the idea of God as if it were a gay and fashionable scarf.' Kafka nodded and smiled. 'And yet it's only a perfectly ordinary tie. As happens always, when transcendence becomes a form of escapism.'

*

On the fourth page of the yellow flyleaves in my copy of the book *A Country Doctor*, there is the following note: 'Literature strives to present things in pleasing, attractive light. But the poet is forced to elevate things into the realm of truth, clarity, and permanence. Literature aims at comfort. But the poet is a seeker after happiness, and that is everything rather than comfortable.'

I do not know whether this is a record of some comment of Kafka's or my own recorded version of the gist of one of our conversations.

*

My schoolfellow, Ernst Lederer, gave me an anthology of expressionist poetry: *The Twilight of Mankind – Symphony of Today's Poetry*. My father, who often looked at what I was reading, said: 'That isn't verse. It's verbal mincemeat.'

I protested: 'That's not fair. It's simply that modern poetry employs a new language.'

'Agreed!' said my father. 'New grass grows every spring. But this grass is indigestible. It's verbal barbed wire. I'll have another look at the book.'[16]

A few days later I spoke to Kafka on my way to my father's department on the first floor of the Workmen's Accident Insurance Institution. After exchanging greetings, he presented me with the expressionist anthology and said reproachfully: 'Why have you scared your father with this book? Your father is an upright, honourable man, with a wealth of valuable experience, but he has no feeling for this kind of trifling with the collapse of logical expression.'

'So you think it's a bad book?'

'I didn't say that.'

'A confection of empty words?'

'No. On the contrary; the book's a frighteningly authentic proof of disintegration. Each of its authors only speaks for himself. They write as if language was their own personal property. But language is only lent to the living, for an undefined period. All we have is the use of it. In reality it belongs to the dead and to those who are still unborn. One must be careful in one's possession of it. That is what the writers in this book have forgotten. They are language destroyers. That is a grave offence. An offence against language is always an offence against feeling and against the mind, a darkening of the world, a breath of the ice age.'

'Yet it's always done in the heat of burning passion!'

'Only verbally. It's a kind of Couéism.'

'It's a betrayal,' I burst out. 'These people pretend to be something that they're not.'

'And so? What's unusual in that?' – His face had a fascinating look of pity, patience and forgiveness. – 'How often is injustice committed in the name of justice? How often does damnation fly the flag of enlightenment? How often does a fall disguise itself as a rise? We can see it all now quite properly. The war didn't only burn and tear the world, but also lit it up. We can see that it is a labyrinth built by men themselves, an icy machine world, whose comforts and apparent purposefulness increasingly emasculate and dishonour us. That is clear in this book which your father lent me. These poets whimper lyrics like freezing children, or wail ecstatically like fanatical fetish worshippers, who strain their words and their limbs all the more, the less they believe in the idols before which they dance.'

*

When my friend Alfred Kämpf from Altsattl on the Eger came to Prague to prepare for his further studies, I trudged with him through Prague's streets, palaces, museums and churches in order to familiarize him with the city I loved. On one of our walks, Alfred surprised me by announcing: 'All this rich gothic and baroque decoration and ornament has only one significance; to disguise the utility, the purely functional aspect, of the various buildings. One is meant to forget the functional, and with it one's own relation to nature and to the world. Beauty divorced from purpose is intended to give men a sense of freedom. An aesthetic culture of ornamental decoration is a school of training in which civilized man turns his back on the human ape within him.' Alfred's words made a tremendous impression on me. I wrote them down at home, and later repeated them word by word to Franz Kafka, who listened to me with half-closed eyes. At that time I had no idea that a long time previously he had written the *Report for an Academy* in which he had described the 'humanization' of a monkey. So I was somewhat disappointed when he said: 'Your friend is right. The civilized world depends for the most part on the effects of successful training procedures. That is what culture means. In the light of Darwinism, man's evolution looks like a monkey's fall from grace. But an organism cannot completely divorce itself from its existential basis.' I answered with a smile: 'A bit of the old monkey's tail still remains.'

'Yes,' agreed Kafka. 'One can evade one's own "I" with great difficulty. The desire for a clear-cut definition of the stage which has to be overcome always leads to intellectual exaggeration and so to repeated disillusionments. Yet this particularly is the most striking expression of the hunger for truth. Men only discover themselves in the dark mirror of tragedy. But by then it's already over.'

'The monkey dies!' I exclaimed impudently.

But Kafka, with an indescribably tender smile, shook his head to and fro in disagreement.

'How could that be? Dying is an exclusively human affair. For that reason, all men die. But the monkey continues to live on in the whole human race. The "I" is nothing else except a cage from the past, its bars entwined with perpetual dreams of the future.'

*

I greeted Kafka on his return from a short visit to his brother-in-law in the country.

'So now we are at home again.'

Kafka smiled sadly.

'At home? I live with my parents. That is all. It is true I have a small room of my own, but that is not a home, only a place of refuge, where I can hide my inner turmoil, only in order to fall all the more headlong into its clutches.'

*

At Kafka's shortly before noon.

He stood at the closed window. With raised hand, he leaned against the window frame. Two paces behind him stood S., a minor official with small bleary eyes, a comical lump of a nose, red-veined hamster cheeks and a rumpled reddish beard. As I entered, S. asked anxiously: 'So you have no idea how the reorganization of our department will turn out?'

'No,' said Kafka, greeted me with a nod of the head, pointed to the visitor's chair beside his desk, and continued: 'All I know is that the reorganization will throw everything into confusion. But don't be alarmed! You won't rise or fall as a result. In the end, everything will be as it was.' In response, the official caught his breath: 'So you think, Herr Doktor, that once again they'll overlook my merits.'

'Yes, that must be assumed.' – Kafka seated himself at his desk. 'After all, the Board will not reduce its own importance. That would be absurd.' S. went red in the face. 'That's shameful! It's so unfair. The whole place ought to be blown up.'

Kafka huddled together, looked up anxiously at S. and said gently: 'You don't really want to destroy the source of your income, do you? Or do you?' 'No,' answered S. apologetically. 'I didn't mean that. You know me, Kafka, I'm a perfectly harmless man, but this reorganization, the perpetual uncertainty in the office, turns my stomach. I had to clear the air. What I just said was only words – '

Kafka interrupted him: 'That's the great danger. Words prepare the way for deeds to come, detonate future explosions.'

'That's not what I intended,' protested the alarmed official.

'So you say,' replied Kafka with a smile. 'But do you know how it looks to others. Perhaps we're already sitting on a powder barrel, which will translate your wish into reality.'

'I can't believe that.'

'Why not? Look out of the window. There's the explosive already which will blow up our Accident Insurance and every other institution in the neighbourhood.'

The official crooked his stubby finger on his chin – 'You're exaggerating, Herr Doktor. There's no danger from the street. The state is very strong.'

'Yes,' Kafka agreed, 'its strength springs from the people's apathy and their need of peace. But what will happen when we can no longer satisfy them? Then your words of abuse today may turn into a universally valid principle of denigration, for words are magical formulae. They leave fingermarks behind on the brain, which in the twinkling of an eye become the footprints of history. One ought to watch one's every word.'

'Yes, you're right there, Herr Doktor, you're right there,' said the dumbfounded S., and took his leave.

As the door closed, I laughed.

Kafka gave me a razor-sharp look.

'What are you laughing at?'

'The poor chap was terribly comic. He entirely failed to understand you.'

'When one man fails to understand another, he is not terribly comic, but isolated, wretched, cut off.'

I tried to defend myself. 'You were joking.' But Kafka made a slow, negative movement of his head.

'No! What I said to S. was said in all seriousness. Today the entire world is haunted by dreams of reorganization. That can mean all kinds of things. Do you understand?'

'Yes,' I said softly, and felt the blood rush to my face. 'I am insensitive and stupid. Forgive me.'

Kafka, however – throwing back his head – only giggled a little. Then he said benevolently: 'Now it's you who are being – in your own words – terribly comic.' I looked contritely at the ground. 'Yes, I'm a wretched creature.' I rose to my feet.

'What are you doing? Sit down!' – With a sharp jerk he opened a drawer of his desk. 'I brought a whole pile of periodicals for you today.' He smiled and I felt even more ashamed. But I remained seated.

*

Later, on two occasions, I was to see other members of the

staff coming to Kafka to question him about the projected reorganization. Kafka, however, had nothing definite to tell them. This depressed him, because it made such people feel that he was not a friend of the staff but merely a devoted servant of the Insurance Institution. So some of the staff made unpleasant remarks about Counsellor Franz Kafka; in particular, the father of one of my schoolfellows, a certain M., whom I met at Kafka's. 'Well then,' he said, in a voice whose dispassionate tone clearly revealed a feeling of hatred, 'you're saying nothing. That's perfectly natural. The Institution's legal representative can't go against the management. He must keep his mouth shut. Forgive me, Herr Doktor, for speaking so plainly and for disturbing you.'

M. bowed and left.

Kafka's face was carved in wood. His eyes were closed.

'What impertinence!' I said angrily.

'He's not impertinent,' Kafka said gently, and looked at me with dark, sad eyes. 'He's only afraid. So he's unjust. Fear for one's daily bread destroys one's character. That's what life is like.'

I pouted: 'Thank you, but not for me. I'd be ashamed of such a life.'

'Most men indeed don't really live at all,' said Kafka, in a strangely soft voice. 'They cling to life like little polyps to a coral reef. But in doing so men are far worse off than those primitive organisms. For them, there's no firm barrier reef to ward off the breakers. They haven't even a shell of their own to live in. All they can do is to emit an acid stream of bile, which leaves them even weaker and more helpless, because it divides them from their fellows. But what can they do about it?'

Franz Kafka spread out his arms and let them fall helplessly, like a pair of broken wings.

'Should one put out into the sea which gives life to such half-formed creatures? It would only be a protest against one's own life, because one is oneself only one of these wretched little coral insects. All one can do is to practise patience and suppress every single drop of bile that rises up in one. It's the only way not to be ashamed of humanity and of oneself.'

*

In the head office of the legal department, by the window, stood two black, plain writing tables, with their longer sides pushed together. The left-hand one – as seen from the doorway – was Kafka's place of work. Opposite him sat Treml, who bore a close resemblance to the former Austro-Hungarian Foreign Minister, Leopold Graf Berchtold. Kafka's colleague was extremely proud of this. He tried to emphasize the likeness by his beard, his hair style, his tall stiff collar with broad cravat and gold pin, his high-buttoned waistcoat, and affected a superior tone of voice. All this made him unpopular with most of the staff of the Accident Insurance Institution. Among themselves they referred to him as 'the impoverished legal Count'. According to my father, this nickname had been invented by a certain Herr Alois Gütling. As far as I can remember he was a small, elegant, almost impeccably dressed member of the staff, with carefully brushed black hair. Gütling wrote poetry, and also – unless I am mistaken – plays which were never produced, admired Richard Wagner and, as he put it, old German alliteration, and could not bear Treml, because Kafka's closest colleague described Gütling's literary productions, which he had privately printed, with their 'high-flying flickering flames' as 'the epitome of middlebrow verse' inspired by 'traditional, old German, philistine idealism'.

Treml indeed, in addition to his resemblance to Count Berchtold, prided himself on his advanced political and materialist outlook. I often saw on his desk books by Ernst Haeckel, Charles Darwin, Wilhelm Bölsche and Ernst Mach. So it was not surprising that one day, when visiting Kafka, I should meet Herr Gütling, who held in his hand a large, black-bound volume, whose title, printed in gold on the leather spine of the book, he read out:

'*Darwin – The Origin of Species*' – he sighed. 'Well, well, so the Count is looking for his ancestors among the apes.' With a wink, Gütling sought to enlist Kafka's sympathy. But Kafka shook his head vigorously and said, without undue emphasis: 'I don't think that's the case any more. It's no longer a question of the ancestors but of the offspring.'

'What do you mean?' Gütling laid the book on the table. 'Treml's a bachelor!'

'I wasn't talking about Treml, but of mankind in general,' said Kafka, and locked his bony fingers together on his chest. 'If things go on as they are the world will soon be peopled by robots reproducing themselves in series.'

Gütling smiled: 'You exaggerate, Herr Doktor. That's a Utopia.' His glance wavered helplessly between Kafka and me. Then it fixed on the base of Kafka's nose, as Gütling said lightly: 'It's like your *Metamorphosis*. I don't understand such things. Myself, I'm a poet.'

Kafka agreed: 'Yes, you are.'

Gütling raised both hands in protest. 'But only as a side-line! Professionally, I'm only a pretty insignificant official. And for that reason, it's already time for me to go.'

He said goodbye.

After he had left, I asked – as I remember exactly today – with a note of disillusion in my voice: 'You really think he's a poet?' Little green sparks shone in Kafka's eyes. 'Yes, in the literal sense of the word. He is a poet (*Dichter*), a dense (*dichter*) man.'

I smiled: 'You mean, closed up.'

Kafka lifted both hands in denial, as if to turn my smile back on me, and said with a slight note of protest in his voice: 'I didn't say that. He is dense. Reality can't penetrate him. He's completely protected against it.'

'By what?'

'By the rubbish of worn-out words and ideas. They're stronger than thick armour plate. Men hide behind them from Time's whirligigs. For that reason, words are evil's strongest buttress. They are the most reliable preservatives of every passion and every stupidity.'

Kafka arranged the papers on his desk. I watched him relapse into silence, and let the words I had just heard echo within me, while my fingers automatically stroked the book lying before me which Gütling had held in his hand when I entered.

Kafka saw this and said: 'The book belongs to Treml. Please put it on his desk. He'd take it very badly if he didn't find it there.'

I obeyed. Then I asked: 'Is he really interested in such matters?'

'Yes,' Kafka replied. 'He's a student of natural history, biology and chemistry. He wants to penetrate the working of the smallest elements in nature, in order to understand the structural meaning of life. Of course, that is a false track.'

'Why?'

'Because the kind of meaning we can arrive at in this way only offers an inadequate reflection of life. It's Heaven captured in a drop of water, an image which is distorted and blurred by our slightest movement.'

'Do you mean that Truth is always closed to us?'

Kafka was silent. His eyes had become quite small and dark. His prominent Adam's apple moved up and down under the flesh of his throat. For a few moments he contemplated the tips of his fingers as they lay on the desk. Then he said gently: 'God, Life, Truth – they are only different names which we give to one fact.'

I pressed him further: 'But can we grasp it?'

'We experience it,' said Kafka, in a slightly troubled voice. 'The fact, to which we give different names, and which we try to apprehend by various processes of thought, pervades our veins, our nerves, our senses. It is within us. For that reason perhaps it's invisible. What we can really grasp is the mystery, the darkness. God dwells in it. And this is a good thing, because without the protecting darkness, we should try to overcome God. That is man's nature. The Son dethrones the Father. So God must remain hidden in darkness. And because man cannot reach him, he attacks at least the darkness which surrounds the divine. He throws burning brands into the icy night. But the night is elastic like rubber. It throws them back.

And by doing so it endures. The only darkness which passes away is that of the human spirit – the light and shadow of the drop of water.'

*

With Kafka on the quay. Heavily loaded coal trucks on the railway viaduct.

I told him how the children from the street in Karolinentel, where I lived, made excursions, during the last year of the war, to the Zizkaberg, where they jumped on the freight trains moving slowly up the track and threw lumps of coal from the uncovered waggons. Later they collected them and carried them home in the sacks which they had brought with them for that purpose. Once one of my schoolfellows – Karel Benda, cross-eyed, the son of a destitute charwoman – was caught in the wheels and cut to pieces.

Kafka asked: 'You were there?'

'No, I only heard about it from the children.'

'You didn't take part in these children's coaling expeditions?'

'Oh yes! Sometimes I accompanied the coal gangs, as the children called them. But I was only a spectator. I didn't steal any coal. We had enough at home. When I went with the children to the Zizkaberg, I usually sat behind a bush or a tree and only watched from a distance what was going on. Sometimes it was very exciting.'

'The struggle for warmth, which is essential to life, is often very exciting,' said Kafka, sharply accentuating my own words. 'It's a decision between life and death. One can't just be a looker-on. There's no bush or tree to hide behind. Life isn't a Zizkaberg. Anyone can fall under its wheels. And indeed the weak and the poor more quickly than the strong and the rich, who are warm enough at home. Oh yes, weakness often breaks down, even before the wheels have touched it.'

I agreed. 'You are right. The little Benda sometimes sat with me behind a bush. Tears used to run down his cheeks. He was afraid. He didn't want to steal coal. He only came because the other children made fun of him and because once his mother had thrashed him with a carpet-beater because he hadn't brought any coal home.'

'That's it,' cried Kafka, with a sweeping gesture of the hand. 'Your schoolfellow, the little Karel Benda, wasn't torn to pieces by a goods train, but much earlier, by the absence of love in his environment. The road to disaster is harder than its end. It couldn't be otherwise. There isn't much to be gained by an act of violence, such as boldly leaping on a moving goods train seemed to him. One simply collects a few lumps of coal that are quickly burned up. And then one is soon standing shivering in the cold again. Day by day, one loses the strength required to repeat such leaps continually. The fear of failure increases. By that time, it's better to beg. There may be someone who will throw us a few lumps of coal.'

'That's right,' I interrupted. 'The coal gang's expeditions began as a kind of begging. The children stood along the railway lines and beseeched the railwaymen for a lump of coal. Usually the railwaymen flung them one or two pieces. The children only began to jump the trucks when there was no more free coal to be had.'

Kafka again agreed. 'That was it. The children only dared to jump when every prospect of a free gift had disappeared and they were deprived of hope. I see them clearly, driven under the wheels by hopelessness.'

We walked on in silence. Kafka gazed for a short time at the rapidly darkening river. Then he talked about something entirely different.

*

Once after supper I mentioned my afternoon walks with Kafka to my father. He said: 'Kafka personifies patience and kindness. I cannot remember an occasion when there was trouble in the Institution on his account. Yet his approachability is not a sign of weakness or a desire to please. On the contrary; he is easy to get on with because, by being completely fair, just and at the same time understanding towards others, he commands a similar response from everyone around him. People speak freely to him, and if they find it hard to agree with him, they prefer to say nothing rather than disagree. This happens in fact quite often, because Kafka expresses unpopular views which are completely his own and contradict accepted opinion. The people at the Accident Insurance Institution don't always understand him. But all the same they are fond of him. For them, he is some strange kind of saint. But so he is to many others. Not so long ago an old labourer whose leg had been smashed by a crane on a building site said to me: "He's no lawyer. He's a saint." The labourer was to receive only a paltry pension from us. He brought an action against us which was not in the proper legal form. The old man would certainly have lost his case, if at the last moment a well-known Prague lawyer had not visited him and – without being paid a penny by the old man – had not expertly redrafted the labourer's case, so that he helped the poor devil to win it. The lawyer, as I learned later, had been instructed, briefed and paid by Kafka, so that, as the legal representative of the Accident Insurance Institution, he might honourably lose the case against the old labourer.'

I was delighted, but my father looked anxious.

He said: 'It's not the only case which Kafka has conducted in this way. The staff take different views about it. Some admire him. Others say he is a bad lawyer.'

'And you?' I interrupted my father. 'How do you feel?'

My father answered with a helpless gesture.

'Who am I to judge Kafka? For me, he's more than a business colleague. I am very fond of him. Because of that, I'm worried by these campaigns for justice.' His face was overcast as he reached for the coffee cup in front of him.

Later I learned that my father gave Kafka active assistance in those 'campaigns for justice'; that he was really more than a mere business colleague and on various occasions Franz Kafka's trusted accomplice.

When he had replaced his coffee cup in front of him, he said: 'Neighbourly love is often a risky thing; just because of this, it is one of the greatest moral values. Kafka is a Jew, but he is far more capable of Christian love than the dear good Catholics and Protestants in the office. Sooner or later they'll be forced to feel ashamed of this. That could lead to some kind of unpleasantness or other. Men often try to disguise one failing by an even greater one. Some careless member of the staff could quite easily blurt out something about Kafka's campaigns for justice. So Kafka ought to be a little more cautious in his love of his neighbours. You tell him so.'

When I accompanied him home two days later, I told Kafka what my father had said. He was silent for a few moments, and then made the following statement: 'Things are not exactly as your father sees them. There is no contradiction between Christian love of one's neighbour and Judaism. On the contrary! Love of mankind is an ethical achievement of the Jews. Christ was a Jew who brought his message of healing to the whole world. Furthermore, every value – material as well as spiritual – involves a risk. For every value demands protection. But so far as shaming others is concerned, your father is right. One ought not to provoke people. We live in an age which is so possessed by demons, that soon we shall only be able to do goodness and justice in the deepest secrecy, as if it were a crime. War and revolution haven't died down. On the contrary. The freezing of our feelings stokes their fires.'

Kafka's tone offended me, so I said: 'So – as in the Bible – we're in the fiery furnace?'

'Yes,' said Kafka, 'it's a miracle that we survive it.'

I shook my head. 'No, it's perfectly normal. I don't believe in the end of the world.'

Kafka smiled. 'That's your duty. A young man who doesn't believe in tomorrow morning is a traitor to himself. If one wishes to live, one must believe.'

'In what?'

'In the significant interrelation of all things and all moments, in the external existence of life as a single whole, in what is nearest and what is farthest.'

*

I told Kafka about the production of two one-act plays, very different in style, by Walter Hasenclever and Arthur Schnitzler, which I had seen in the New German Theatre.[17]

'The programme was badly balanced,' I said, at the end of my account. 'The expressionism of one play spoilt the realism of the other, and *vice versa*. Probably the production had not allowed enough time for study.'

'Quite possible,' said Kafka. 'The German theatre in Prague is in a very difficult position. Taken as whole, it forms a large complex of financial and human relationships, to which there is no correspondingly large public. It is a pyramid without a base. The actors are subordinate to the producers, who are controlled by the management, which is responsible to the committee of the theatre club. It is a chain which lacks the final link to hold it together. There is no genuine German community here, and therefore no dependable, permanent audience. The German-speaking Jews in the boxes and in the stalls are, after all, not Germans, and the German students who come to Prague and sit in the balcony and the gallery are merely the advance guard of an invading power – not spectators. In such conditions it is naturally impossible to achieve a serious work of art. Their energies are wasted on accidentals. What is left are efforts and exertions which scarcely ever end in a good production. So I never go to the theatre. It is too sad.'

*

In the German Theatre they were performing Walter Hasenclever's play *The Son*.[18]

Franz Kafka said, 'The revolt of the son against the father is one of the primeval themes of literature, and an even older problem in the world. Dramas and tragedies are written about it, yet in reality it is material for comedy. The Irishman Synge was right in realizing this. In his play *The Playboy of the Western World* the son is an adolescent exhibitionist who boasts of having murdered his father. Then along comes the old man and turns the young conqueror of paternal authority into a figure of fun.'

'I see that you are very sceptical about the struggle of the young against the old,' I said.

Kafka smiled.

'My scepticism does not alter the fact that this struggle is usually only shadow boxing.'

'What do you mean – shadow boxing?'

'Age is the future of youth, which sooner or later it must reach. So why struggle? To become old sooner? For a quicker departure?'

The entry of an official interrupted our conversation.

*

In the German Theatre the actor Rudolf Schildkraut[19] from the Hoftheater in Vienna was giving a guest performance in Sholem Asch's play, *The God of Vengeance*. I talked about it to Kafka.

'Rudolf Schildkraut is recognized as a great actor,' said Franz Kafka. 'But is he a great Jewish actor? In my opinion this is doubtful. Schildkraut acts Jewish parts in Jewish plays. But since he does not act exclusively in Jewish for Jews, but in German for everyone, he is not an expressly Jewish actor. He is a borderline case, an intermediary, who gives people an insight into the intimacy of Jewish life. He enlarges the horizons of non-Jews, without illuminating the existence of the Jews themselves. This is only done by the poor Jewish actors who act for Jews in Jewish. By their art they sweep away the deposits of an alien world from the life of the Jews, display in the bright light of day the hidden Jewish face which is sinking into oblivion, and so give them an anchor in the troubles of our time.'

I told him how at the end of the war I had seen two performances by travelling Jewish actors in the little cafe Savoy on the Geisplatz. Kafka was extremely surprised.

'How did you come to be there?'

'With my mother. She lived for a long time in Poland.'

'And what did you think of the theatre?'

I shrugged my shoulders.

'I only remember that I hardly understood the language.

The performance was in dialect. But my mother admired the actors.'

Kafka looked into the distance.

'I used to know the Jewish actors in the Savoy cafe. That was about ten years ago. I also had difficulties with the language. Then I discovered that I understood more Yiddish than I had imagined.'[20]

'My mother spoke fluent Yiddish,' I said proudly. I told him how as a six-year-old child I had been with my mother in the Schwarzgasse in the Jewish quarter of Przemysl. And how out of the ancient houses and the dark little shops men and women ran out and kissed my mother's hand and the hem of her coat, laughed and cried and shouted, 'Our good lady! Our good lady!' I learned later that my mother had hidden many Jews in her house during the pogroms.

Franz Kafka said, when I had finished recounting these memories:

'And I should like to run to those poor Jews of the Ghetto, kiss the hem of their coats, and say not a word. I should be completely happy if only they would endure my presence in silence.'

'Are you so lonely?' I asked.

Kafka nodded.

'Like Kaspar Hauser?' I said.

Kafka laughed.

'Much worse than Kaspar Hauser. I am as lonely as – as Franz Kafka.'

*

On one of our walks, as we passed through some of the narrow alleyways and passages of Prague's Old Town into the modernity of the Graben, my friend Alfred Kämpf said to me: 'Prague is a tragic city. One can see that in its architecture, where the medieval and the modern are intermingled with almost no transition between them. Because of it, the rows of houses have a visionary and dreamlike air. Prague is an expressionist city. Its houses, streets, palaces, churches, museums, bridges, factories, towers, tenements, are the expression in stone of a profound, internal movement. It's not for nothing that the city arms of Prague show an iron fist breaking down the latticed gate of constricting city walls. The day-to-day face of the city conceals a rabid and dramatic will to life, which by destroying the vestiges of the past re-creates new forms of existence over and over again. Yet in itself this implies a decline. Violence calls forth violence. Technical progress will destroy the iron fist. The smell of decay already pervades the present.'

When I reached home, I wrote Kämpf's words in my journal, so that I might read them to Kafka in the Accident Insurance Institution the following day. He listened attentively, and when I replaced the diary in the brief-case on my knee, he drew in his lower lip for a few moments. Then he leaned slowly forward, settled his elbows comfortably on his desk, his face lost its look of strain, and he said carefully in a gentle voice: 'Your friend's words are themselves an iron fist. I can imagine how violently you must stimulate each other. I often find the same thing with my own friends. They are so eloquent, that they are always forcing me to think for myself.' He coughed in his own particular way, that was like the soft rustle of paper, let his head sink and said, with a concentrated look at the floor: 'Not only Prague – the whole world is tragic. The iron fist of technology destroys all protecting walls. That's not expressionism. It's the nakedness of daily life. We are driven towards truth like criminals to the seat of judgement.'

'Why? Do we offend public order? Do we provoke breaches of the peace?'

The slightly scolding tone of my questions alarmed me, so that I instinctively put my thumb to my mouth and tried to guess Kafka's reaction from his expression. But he looked over me, and over all things, into infinity, and yet at the same time he registered every word of my question.

He said: 'Yes, we are disturbers of order and of peace. That is our original sin. We set ourselves above nature. We are not content to die and to survive merely as members of a species.

Each of us wishes to preserve and possess his life for as long as possible as an individual organism. This is a rejection, by which we forfeit life.'

'I don't understand,' I said frankly. 'It's after all natural that we should wish to live and not to die. What extraordinary offence do we then commit?' My voice was lightly ironic, but Franz Kafka did not seem to notice. He said very calmly: 'We attempt to set our own narrow world above the infinite. Thereby we disturb the rhythm of things. That is our original sin. All phenomena in the cosmos and on the earth move in cycles, like the heavenly bodies, it is an eternal repetition; man alone, the concrete living organism, runs a direct course between life and death. For man there is no personal return. He only follows a declining path. So he breaks the cosmic order. That's original sin.' I interrupted him: 'But he can't help it! It can't be a sin to do what is imposed on us by our fate.'

Kafka slowly turned his face towards me. I saw his large grey eyes: they were dark and opaque. His whole face was suffused by a deep, stony calm. Only his slightly protuberant upper lip trembled a little. Or was it a shadow?

'Do you wish to protest against God?'

I looked at the ground. Silence. The sound of a voice behind the wall. Then Franz Kafka said: 'To deny original sin is to deny God and man. Perhaps man is first given freedom by mortality. How can we know?'

*

While walking on the Altstädter Ring we discussed Max Brod's play, *The Forger*. I explained to Kafka my ideas about its production. In our discussion we came to the point in the play where the entry of a woman changes the whole situation. My idea was that the characters on the stage should fall back slowly as she entered, but Kafka did not agree.

'They must all fall back as if struck by lightning,' he said.

'That would be too theatrical,' I objected.

But Franz Kafka shook his head.

'So it should be. Actors ought to be theatrical. To create the desired effect their emotions and actions must be larger than the feelings and actions of their audience. If the theatre is to affect life, it must be stronger, more intense than ordinary life. That is the law of gravity. In shooting one must aim higher than the mark.'

*

The Prague Ständetheater was performing the revolutionary play, *Tanja*, by Ernst Weiss, who was one of Max Brod's circle of friends.[21]

When I told Kafka about the performance, which I had seen, he said:

'The finest scene is the dream scene with Tanja's child. The theatre makes its strongest effect, when it makes unreal things real. Then the stage becomes a periscope for the soul, illuminating reality from within.'

*

My school friend, George Kraus, a relation of the composer Gustav Mahler, lent me two books by the French writer, Henri Barbusse: *Le Feu* and *Clarté*.[22]

Kafka, for whom I had in fact borrowed the books, said: 'Fire, as an image of war, corresponds to the truth. Clarity, however, is a title for dreams and wishes. The war led us into a maze of distorting mirrors. We stumble from one false perspective into another, the bewildered victims of false prophets and charlatans, whose recipes for happiness only close one's eyes and ears, so that we fall through the mirrors, like trap doors, from one disaster to another.'

I must confess that at the moment I could not fully understand what Kafka meant. But I didn't want to stand there as if I were feeble-witted, so I took refuge in the question: 'What brought us into such a situation? And what keeps us in it? Somehow we must have entered the hall of mirrors of our own volition. What made us do it?'

'Our superhuman greed and vanity, the *hubris* of our will to power. We struggle to achieve values which are not really values at all, in order to destroy things on which our whole existence as human beings depends. Therein lies a confusion which drags us into the mire and destroys us.'

*

I took with me to the Workmen's Accident Insurance Institution a book, *The Two-headed Nymph*, by Kasimir Edschmid, who in one chapter, 'Theodor Daübler and the Abstract School', discussed Franz Kafka.[23]

'Have you seen this?' I asked.

Franz Kafka nodded.

'My attention was drawn to it.'

'And what do you think of it?'

Franz Kafka shrugged his shoulders and made a helpless gesture with his right hand.

'Edschmid speaks of me as if I were an engineer. Whereas I am only a very mediocre, clumsy draughtsman. He claims that I introduce miracles into ordinary events. That is, of course, a serious error on his part. The ordinary is itself a miracle! All I do is to record it. Possibly, I also illuminate matters a little, like the lighting on a half-dark stage. And yet that is not true! In fact, the stage is not dark at all. It is filled with daylight. Therefore men close their eyes, and see so little.'

'There is often a painful difference between perception and reality,' I said.

Kafka nodded.

'All is struggle, effort. Only those deserve love and life who have to conquer them each day.'

There was a short pause. Then he added softly with an ironical smile:

'Says Goethe.'

'Johann Wolfgang von Goethe?'

A quick nod.

'Goethe says practically everything that matters to us human beings.'

'My friend Alfred Kämpf told me that Oswald Spengler had taken the doctrine of *The Decline of the West* from Goethe's *Faust*.'

'That is perfectly possible,' said Franz Kafka. 'Many so-called scholars transfer the world of the poet to another, scholarly, plane, and so achieve fame and importance.'

*

My father took a passionate interest in all forms of carpentry and had his own little carpenter's workshop in the attic, with a joiner's bench and a small circular saw; he was always dreaming of acquiring a turner's lathe. He had a friend of many years' standing whom he greatly admired, a tax official named Jan Cerný. But taxation was only the way he earned his living. His real interest in life was the craft of the Italian violin makers. In order to understand their art, he occupied his spare time for many years in research into varnishes, wood, spatial volumes, and the construction of old Italian, German and Czech violins. He studied chemistry, history and acoustics. He possessed a considerable collection of stringed instruments, specialized electrical measuring apparatus and of course a well-equipped workshop with two turner's lathes which fascinated my father. He often went straight to Cerný from his work, and once took me with him to act as a piano accompanist to the latest work of the fanatical violin maker.

I remember the day exactly – the beginning of May, rain – but I have forgotten Cerný's address at the time. Yet my memory has retained exactly the atmosphere of the 'violin laboratory', as my father called Cerný's house.

On entering the house, one felt one was in any minor civil servant's home. But that was only a deceptive appearance which camouflaged the existence of some extraordinary alchemist's cave. The division between its owner's interests in life was revealed in the arrangements of Cerný's home. To the left of the small narrow entrance hall was a small kitchen and adjoining it a rather sombre living-room. This was the stage for the completely petit-bourgeois existence of Herr Cerný and his wife Agnes. But immediately opposite was the showroom for his devouring passion, a large whitewashed room, on whose walls hung strange diagrams, sheets of graphs, a few violins and long racks filled with an array of chemical retorts, boxes, lamps, measuring instruments and large jars containing brushes. There were two windows before which stood a joiner's bench and a large black piano. On the left-hand wall stood two lathes, a tall bookshelf piled higgledy-piggledy with files and a table on which stood a gas cooker. Opposite, on the right of the door, on a dusty iron clothes-rack hung a dirty painter's smock, a pair of old worn paint-bespattered trousers and a bowler hat turned rust-brown by dust. On the wall beside it was a row of small shelves of varying length. The whole room was filled with a penetrating odour of oil, glue and tobacco, which tickled my nostrils unpleasantly. But my father's eyes were shining. He said: 'This is a real workshop, isn't it? Do you see the lathes?'

I only said: 'Hm.'

Then we went into the living-room-bedroom, with its green plush furniture, a round table, and two coffin-shaped marital beds. Frau Cerný served coffee with cream and a tall egg-yellow cake. The coffee smelt of petrol and the cake crackled like sand or emery paper between one's teeth. It's possible, however, that this only seemed so to me because I was completely overcome by my impression of the violin laboratory.

To exorcize it, I afterwards wrote a story which I called *The Music of Silence*, inspired by what Cerný had said during our visit.

He said: 'Life means to be the object and the cause of motion. But motion only partially reveals itself as spatial change. To a much greater extent, the motion we experience proceeds without any change of place. Everything that lives is in flux. Everything that lives emits sound. But we only perceive a part of it. We do not hear the circulation of the blood, the growth and decay of our bodily tissue, the sound of our chemical processes. But our delicate organic cells, the fibres of brain and nerves and skin are impregnated with these inaudible sounds. They vibrate in response to their environment. This is the foundation of the power of music. We can set free these profound emotional vibrations. In order to do so, we employ musical instruments, in which the decisive factor is their own inner sound potential. That is to say: what is decisive is not the strength of the sound, or its tonal colour, but its hidden character, the intensity with which its musical power affects the nerves. This is the fundamental problem of every musical instrument and every instrument maker. He must try and endow his instrument with the highest possible degree of tonal intensity. That is to say: he must construct instruments which elevate into human consciousness vibrations which are otherwise inaudible and unperceived. The instrument maker's problem is therefore that of bringing silence to life. He must uncover the hidden sound of silence.'

On the basis of such ideas, I wrote my fantasy of an instrument maker who by means of new sound equipment gave his listeners entirely novel and entrancing sensations which exceeded anything they had previously experienced; their intensity increased until they became a pain which lacerated the nerves of the listeners and after a time finally drove the instrument maker mad.

I gave the story to Kafka, who after a few days said to me with a smile: 'I know the acoustic devil's kitchen of which you have written. I have visited Herr Cerný several times with your father. We planed a few shelves there and had to turn a few things on the lathes. Herr Cerný expounded his theory of the musical power of silence and showed us his remarkable new violin with the air vents in the side walls. He even played us something but I don't understand such matters. As far as I can remember the new violin had a brittle, slightly metallic tone. That was the only impression Cerný's musical instruments made on me. I said so to him. Perhaps I hurt his feelings because afterwards he was not so friendly to me as he had been. So I've never been there again.'

'What do you think of Cerný's theory of silence?'

'It's not new. Like X-rays, there are of course also sound waves which are inaudible to the human ear. A Frenchman – I don't remember his name any more – demonstrated by a series of clever experiments that insects communicate with each other by sound waves which cannot be heard by the human ear. So why shouldn't the limits of sensitivity be enlarged? A man's not a stone. But even a stone is capable of change. A mineral decays, breaks up, is transformed into a geometrically perfect crystal. Man is not only a work of nature but is also his own artefact, a daemon who continually breaks through the established frontiers and makes visible what was hitherto in darkness.'

'So you think Cerný should be taken seriously?'

'Of course! One should take everyone seriously. Everyone has his own particular demand for happiness. Whether it's a question of a stroke of genius or only a piece of harmless eccentricity – only time can tell.'

'But do you think that Time is just?' I asked sceptically. 'Time is Janus-headed. It has two faces – '

'It even has two natures,' said Kafka with a smile. 'It is both duration, resistance to decay, and the possibility of a future, the hope of a new duration, change, which endows every phenomenon with conscious existence.'

*

I was with Kafka in his office. I had with me Christian Morgenstern's *Songs of the Gallows*.

'Do you know his serious poems?' Kafka asked me. '*Time and Eternity? Steps?*'

'No, I had no idea that he wrote serious poems.'

'Morgenstern is a terribly serious poet. His poems are so serious that in *Songs of the Gallows* he has to save himself from his own inhuman seriousness.'

*

The German poet from Prague, Johannes Urzidil,[24] collected and published the poems of his dead, scarcely twenty-year-old friend. I asked Franz Kafka whether he had known the dead friend. I no longer remember his reply, except for his final words.

'He was one of those unhappy young men who had lost himself among the centenarian Jews of the cafés; and died. What else could he do? In our time the cafés are the catacombs of the Jews. Without light and without love. Not everyone can bear that.'

*

I first came across the name of the mysterious foundling, Kaspar Hauser, who appeared in Nuremberg in the year 1828, in the poems of Georg Trakl. Later Lydia Holzner[25] lent me Jacob Wassermann's long novel, *Caspar Hauser or The Sluggish Heart*.

On that occasion Franz Kafka remarked:

'Wassermann's Caspar Hauser has long ceased to be a foundling. He is now legitimized, settled in the world, registered with the police, a taxpayer. Moreover, he has abandoned his old name. He is now called Jacob Wassermann, German novelist and householder. In secret he also suffers from sluggishness of heart, which gives him pangs of conscience. But he works it up into well-paid prose, and so all is for the best.'

*

My father loved Altenberg's poems in prose. Whenever he found one of these little sketches in the newspaper, he cut it out and preserved the cutting carefully in a special folder.

When I told Franz Kafka this, he smiled, leaned forward, pressed his clasped hands between his knees, and said very softly:

'That is beautiful. That is very beautiful. I have always liked your father so much. At first sight he seems so cold and prosaic. One thinks he is merely an industrious and able official. Yet when one knows him better, one discovers under his deceptive appearance a living spring of warm humanity. Your father – in spite of his knowledge – has a lively creative fantasy. And so he loves poetry. For Peter Altenberg is really a poet. His little anecdotes reflect his entire life. And every step, every gesture he makes guarantees the veracity of his words. Peter Altenberg is a genius of trivialities, a strange idealist, who discovers the beauties of the world like cigarette-ends in the ashtrays of cafés.'

*

Directly after the First World War the most successful German novel was Gustav Meyrink's *The Golem*. Franz Kafka gave me his opinion of the book.

'The atmosphere of the old Jewish quarter of Prague is wonderfully reproduced.'

'Do you still remember the old Jewish quarter?'

'As a matter of fact, I came when it had already disappeared. But . . .'

Kafka made a gesture with his left hand, as if to say, 'What good did it do?' His smile replied, 'None'.

Then he continued, 'In us all it still lives – the dark corners, the secret alleys, shuttered windows, squalid courtyards, rowdy pubs, and sinister inns. We walk through the broad streets of the newly built town. But our steps and our glances are uncertain. Inside we tremble just as before in the ancient streets of our misery. Our heart knows nothing of the slum clearance which has been achieved. The unhealthy old Jewish town within us is far more real than the new hygienic town around us. With our eyes open we walk through a dream: ourselves only a ghost of a vanished age.'

*

In a second-hand bookshop I found a Czech translation of Leon Bloy's book, *The Blood of the Poor*.[26]

Franz Kafka was extremely interested in my discovery. He said:

'I know a book of Leon Bloy's against anti-semitism, *Salvation through the Jews*. In it a Christian takes the Jews – like poor relations – under his protection. It is extremely interesting. And then – Bloy can curse. That is something quite extraordinary. Bloy has a fire which reminds one of the fervour of the prophets.

What am I saying; Bloy is much better at cursing. That is easily understandable, because his fire is nourished by all the filth of modern times.'

*

Franz Kafka gave me a short essay on Sören Kierkegaard by Carl Dallago.[27] He said on this occasion:

'Kierkegaard faces the problem, whether to enjoy life aesthetically or to experience it ethically. But this seems to me a false statement of the problem. The Either–Or exists only in the head of Sören Kierkegaard. In reality one can only achieve an aesthetic enjoyment of life as a result of humble ethical experience. But this is only a personal opinion of the moment, which perhaps I shall abandon after closer inquiry.'

*

Sometimes with Franz Kafka I met Hans Klaus, whom I had already met at school, but until then had not known well, because he was several years older than me. In addition, he was already well known as the author of a number of poems and stories. Compared with him I was merely an immature little schoolboy. Yet it seemed to me that Franz Kafka talked to me more as a friend than to Klaus. I was pleased by this, and at the same time ashamed of myself.

'Are you only a child to Kafka?' I asked myself, and immediately reassured myself: 'You probably only imagine that he is more friendly to you than to Klaus.'

I had no peace. So one day I turned to Kafka as I accompanied him from the office along the Altstädter Ring.

'What do you think – am I vain?'

Kafka was astonished.

'What made you think of such a question?'

'It seems to me that you are more friendly to me than to Klaus. That makes me happy. It makes me very happy. At the same time I tell myself that these are merely the whispers of vanity.'

Kafka took me by the arm.

'You are a child.'

My chin began to tremble.

'Look, I always think that you are so good to me only because I am still a foolish, immature child.'

'For me you are a young man,' said Franz Kafka. 'You have future possibilities which others have already lost. People mean so much to you that you have to watch yourself very closely, in order not to lose yourself. Certainly I am more friendly to you than to Klaus. After all, I speak to my own past when I speak to you. One cannot help being friendly. And then; you are younger than Klaus, and so you need more understanding and love.'

*

From that day on my relations with Klaus altered. We became fast friends. He introduced me to his literary companions, the doctor Rudolf Altschul and the architect Konstantin Ahne, who published poems under the name of Hans Tine Kanton.

We called on each other, went together to the theatre, made excursions, lent each other books, debated with each other and – admired each other.

Thus a group called *Protest* was founded, which arranged an evening of readings of its own works in the Mozarteum.

We wished to give the audience something by Franz Kafka; but he had strongly forbidden it.

'You must be mad!' he said to me. 'A protest which is licensed and approved by the police! It is both absurd and sad. It is worse than real revolt, because it is only a sham outburst. But I in any case am no protestant. I wish to accept everything and bear it patiently, but I will not accept a public exhibition of this kind.'

I hastened to explain that I had nothing in common with Altschul, Klaus, and Ahne. The trio disbanded. Kafka meant more to me than my own vanity.[28]

*

When, some months later, Hans Klaus and I quarrelled, I told
Kafka, who listened quietly, then shrugged his shoulders and
said:

'Now you would like to have some advice from me. But I am
not a good adviser. All advice seems to me to be at bottom a
betrayal. It is a cowardly retreat in face of the future, which is
the touchstone of our present. But only those fear to be put to
the proof who have a bad conscience. They are the ones who
do not fulfil the tasks of the present. Yet who knows precisely
what his task is? No one. So that every one of us has a bad
conscience, which he tries to escape by going to sleep as quickly
as possible.'

I remarked that Johannes R. Becher in one of his poems
describes sleep as a friendly visitation by death.[29]

Kafka nodded.

'That is true. Perhaps my insomnia is only a kind of fear of
the visitor whom I must pay for my life.'

*

The poet Hans Klaus gave me a little book: *Tubutsch*, by Albert
Ehrenstein, with twelve drawings by Oskar Kokoschka. Kafka
saw the book, I lent it to him, and he returned it to me on my
next visit to his office.

'Such a small book and so much noise,' he remarked. '*Mankind Shrieks*. Do you know it?'

'No.'

'It is – I think – the title of a book of poems by Albert
Ehrenstein.'[30]

'So you know him well?'

'Well?' said Kafka, and shrugged his shoulders in denial.
'One never knows the living. The present is change and transformation. Albert Ehrenstein is one of today's generation. He
is a child lost and crying in the night.'

'What do you think of Kokoschka's drawings?'

'I do not understand them. Drawing derives from to draw,
to describe, to show. All they show me is the painter's internal
confusion and disorder.'

'I saw his large picture of Prague at the Expressionist exhibition in the Rudolfinum.'

Kafka turned his left hand, which was lying on the table, palm upwards.

'The big one – with the green cupola of the Niklaskirche in the centre?'

'Yes, that is the one.'

He bowed his head.

'In that picture the roofs are flying away. The cupolas are umbrellas in the wind. The whole city is flying in all directions. Yet Prague still stands – despite all internal conflicts. That is the miracle.'

*

I had set to music two poems from Johannes Schlaf's collection, *Spring*. I sent a copy to the author of the words. Johannes Schlaf thanked me in a long handwritten letter which I showed to Franz Kafka.

He laughed, as he gave me the letter back across the writing-table.

'Schlaf is so touching. We visited him when we were in Weimar with Max Brod. He would not mention literature or art. All his attention was concentrated on overthrowing the existing solar system.'

'Not long ago I saw a long book by Schlaf in which he claimed that the centre of the earth was the centre of the cosmos.'[31]

'Yes, that was his idea even then, and he tried to convince us of its truth by means of his own special theory of sun spots. He took us to the window of his modest dwelling and showed us the sun with the assistance of a schoolboy's antiquated telescope.'

'You must have laughed.'

'Why? The fact that he dared to do battle with science and the cosmos armed with this ridiculous object inherited from ancient times was so absurd and so affecting at the same time that we almost believed him.'

'What prevented you?'

'As a matter of a fact, the coffee. It was bad. We had to leave.'

*

I repeated Reimann's amusing story about Kurt Wolff, the Leipzig publisher, who at eight o'clock in the morning rejected a translation of Rabindranath Tagore, and two hours later sent the firm's reader to the central post office to reclaim the rejected manuscript, because in the meanwhile he had seen in the paper that Tagore had won the Nobel Prize.

'Odd that he should have refused Tagore,' said Franz Kafka slowly. 'Tagore is after all not very different from Kurt Wolff. India and Leipzig, the distance between is only apparent. In reality Tagore is only a German in disguise.'

'A schoolmaster, perhaps?'

'A schoolmaster?' repeated Kafka gravely, drew down the corners of his tight-pressed lips, and slowly shook his head. 'No, not that, but he could be a Saxon – like Richard Wagner.'

'Mysticism in Tyrolean dress?'

'Something like that.'

We laughed.

*

I lent Kafka a German translation of the Indian religious text, the *Bhagavad Gita*.[32]

Kafka said, 'Indian religious writings attract and repel me at the same time. Like a poison, there is something both seductive and horrible in them. All these Yogis and sorcerers rule over the life of nature not because of their burning love of freedom but because of a concealed and icy hatred of life. The source of Indian religious devotions is a bottomless pessimism.'

I recalled Schopenhauer's interest in Indian religious philosophy.

Kafka said, 'Schopenhauer is an artist in language. That is the source of his thinking. For the language alone, one must not fail to read him.'

*

Franz Kafka laughed, when he saw me with a little book of poems by Michael Mareš.33

'I know him,' he said. 'He is a fierce anarchist whom they endure as a curiosity in the *Prager Tagblatt*.'

'You don't take the Czech anarchists seriously?'

Kafka smiled apologetically.

'That is very hard. These people, who call themselves anarchists, are so nice and friendly, that one has to believe every word they say. At the same time – and by reason of the same qualities – one cannot believe that they are really such world destroyers as they claim.'

'So you know them personally?'

'A little. They are very nice, jolly people.'

*

A few days later I learned some interesting details about his relations with the anarchists.

Kafka and I were walking from the Altstädter Ring through the Geistgasse and past the Church of the Brothers of Mercy, to the Moldau. There we turned to the left, crossed the square in front of the Parliament House and sauntered along the Kreuzherrengasse to the Charles Bridge, where we entered the Karlsgasse and so returned to the Altstädter Ring.

During our walk we met various passers-by of no particular interest. On the corner of the Ekidi and the Karlsgasse, however, we almost collided with two ladies of a quite unmistakable kind. One had an almost circular, white-powdered face, under a great bird's nest of red hair, while the other, somewhat smaller, had a painted mousey face and the slightly swarthy complexion of a gypsy.

We stood against the wall, but the two women in any case took no notice of us. They were too deeply occupied with an event which had occurred shortly before.

'He took me by the scruff of the neck and shot me out of the door,' the darker one whined.

Red-Head bleated triumphantly: 'What did I tell you? You're not allowed inside the place.'

'What rubbish! The Altstädter Café's open to the public like any other café.'34

'But not to you. You're not allowed in. Not since you jabbed fat Emma in the stomach.'

'She deserved it. The old sow.'

'Yes, so she is. But the porter's her old man. That's why he kicked you out.'

'What a ravachol! The way he held me – '

The pair vanished into an alley.

We walked on in the opposite direction.

'Did you hear that last word?' Kafka asked.

'You mean ravachol?'

'Yes. Do you know what it means?'

'Yes, of course! Ravachol's Prague slang. It means something like violent brute, bully, ruffian.'

'Yes,' said Kafka. 'At first that's what I too took the word to mean. But in fact it's a French surname which in its Czech form has with the passage of time become a Czech noun indicating a specific characteristic.'

'Something like Solomon or Herod?'

'Yes, more or less,' said Kafka. 'Ravachol was a French anarchist. In fact his real name was Franz Augustin Königstein. But he didn't like the German name. So he adopted the French version of his mother's name – Ravaschool. The simple Prague newspaper reader, however, pronounced it as it looked to him in print – Ravachol. The Press took an interest in him for quite a long time.'

'When was that?'

'That was between 1891 and 1894. I was a small boy then, and our Czech nursery maid took me to school every day across the Altstädter Ring and through the Teingasse to the Fleischmarkt. After lessons the maid usually waited for me at the school door. But sometimes she was late, or school ended earlier than usual. I was always glad when that happened. I always joined a gang of the biggest guttersnipes in the class and with them I marched off to the Ziegengasse in the opposite direction from which I might expect the maid to come, and nearly every evening there was some kind of rough-house.'

'In which you certainly took no part,' I said without thinking, in a voice of the deepest conviction, because I really could not imagine Kafka as a schoolboy being involved in any kind of fighting.

But Kafka laughed, threw his head back and said: 'I didn't take part in such street fights? Though I hadn't any experience of fighting, and at heart I was frightened, I always pressed into the thick of them in order to convince my schoolfellows that I wasn't the spoiled mother's boy that they used to call me. And also I didn't want to seem a little Jewish weakling. But I didn't convince them, because usually I was beaten up. I often came home after outings in tears, dirty, the buttons off my jacket and my collar torn. The house was here.'

Kafka stood in the Kleiner Ring near the baroque entrance of the Schubert House and with a brief nod of the head indicated the medieval house *Minuta* which juts out from the front of the adjoining houses and divides the Altstädter Ring from the Kleiner Ring. 'My parents lived on the upper storey. By day they worked in the shop. They left the housekeeping to the cook and the nursery maid. They were always very upset when I returned crying, torn and dirty from one of those street fights. The maid wrung her hands, cried, and threatened to tell my parents about my behaviour. But she never did. On the contrary! The cook and the maid together destroyed the evidence of my battles as quickly as they could. Once while they were doing so the cook muttered: "You're a ravachol." I didn't know what she meant. I asked but she only said: "That's what you are. You're a real ravachol." She thus included me in a class of humanity which was quite unknown to me. She made me a part of a dark mystery which made me tremble. I was a ravachol! The word affected me like a verbal spell which evoked an unbearable tension. In order to escape from it, one evening while my parents were playing cards I asked what a ravachol was. Without looking up from his cards, my father replied: "A criminal, a murderer." I must have looked extremely surprised and stupid, because my mother

asked me anxiously: "Where did you hear that word?" I
stammered some reply. The knowledge that the cook had
recognized a murderer in me paralysed my tongue. My mother
looked at me inquiringly in the face. She was already about to
lay down her cards and subject me to interrogation. But my
father wanted to go on playing cards and said rather testily:
"Where would he have heard that word? In school or on the
streets somewhere. People are talking about the fellow every-
where." My mother replied: "Yes, they make much too much
fuss about such riff-raff." Then my father slapped a card –
Trumps! – on the table and I crept completely dumbfounded
from the room. The next day I was feverish. The doctor was
summoned and diagnosed an inflammation of the throat. He
prescribed some medicine or other. When the maid went to the
chemist's with the prescription, the cook sat on my bed. She
was a large, fat, good-natured person whom we called Frau
Anna. Now she stroked my hands which were lying on the
counterpane and said: "Don't be afraid, you'll soon be well" –
But I hid my hands under the counterpane and asked: "Why
am I a criminal?" The cook opened her eyes wide at me and
said: "A criminal? Who told you that?" – "You! You yourself!" – "Me?" – "Frau Anna" pressed her fists to her massive
bosom and said indignantly: "That's completely untrue!" But
I said: "It's the absolute truth. You called me a ravachol. That's
a criminal. My parents said so." – Then "Frau Anna" clapped
her hands above her head and smilingly explained: "Yes, I did
say ravachol. But I didn't mean any harm. Ravachol – it's just
something people say. I didn't mean to insult you." – She
stroked my cheek to comfort me. But I turned my face to the
wall. Immediately afterwards the maid came with the medicine.
The name of ravachol was never spoken again amongst us but
it remained within me like a thorn, or rather like the broken-off
point of a needle which circulates about the body. The inflammation of the throat disappeared, but subjectively I remained a
stricken invalid, a ravachol. Outwardly nothing had changed.
People treated me in the same way as before, but I knew that
I was an Ishmael, a criminal, in short – a ravachol. I took no

further part in the other boys' street fights. I always went home like a good boy with the nursery maid. People were not going to say of me that I was a ravachol.'

'But that's absurd!' I cried without thinking. 'Time must have washed it all away.'

'On the contrary!' Kafka gave a painful smile. 'Nothing sticks so fast in the mind as a groundless sense of guilt, because – since it has no real foundation – one cannot eliminate it by any form of repentance or redemption. So I remained a ravachol even when I had apparently long forgotten the incident with the cook and had learned the real meaning of the word.'

'You studied Ravachol's life?'

'Yes. And not only Ravachol's but the lives of various other anarchists. I went deeply into the lives and ideas of Godwin, Proudhon, Stirner, Bakunin, Kropotkin, Tucker and Tolstoy, frequented various circles and meetings, and devoted much time and money to the subject. In 1910 I took part in the meetings of the anarchist *Club of the Young* which, disguised as a mandolin club, met in the inn *Zum Kanonenkreuz* in Karolinenthal.[35] Max Brod sometimes came with me to the meetings, though he had little sympathy with them. He regarded them as a kind of youthful aberration. But for me they were a very serious matter. I followed in the footsteps of Ravachol. They led me later to Erich Mühsam,[36] Arthur Holitscher,[37] and the Viennese anarchist Rudolf Gassman, who called himself Pierre Ramuz and edited the journal *Wealth for All*. They all attempted to realize the happiness of mankind without the aid of grace. But – ,' Kafka lifted both arms like a pair of broken wings and let them fall helplessly, 'I could not march shoulder to shoulder with them for long. I stuck to Max Brod, Felix Weltsch and Oskar Baum.[38] They are closer to me.'

He came to a halt. We had reached the house where he lived. He smiled wistfully at me for one or two seconds. Then he said, 'All Jews are – like me – rejected ravachols. I still feel the blows and kicks of the naughty boys on my roundabout way home, but I can't fight any more. I no longer have the strength of youth. And a protective nursery maid? I haven't that either any more.'

He held out his hand. 'It's late. Goodnight.'

*

I brought Kafka a new issue of *Die Fackel*, published by Karl Kraus in Vienna.

'He is marvellous at tearing the journalists to pieces,' he said as he turned the leaves. 'Only a converted poacher could be such a strict keeper.'

'Karl Kraus[39] exposes Georg Kulka, who adapts plays for the Vienna Burgtheater, as a plagiarist.[40] What do you think of that?'

'That is nothing. Just a little failure of the brain tracts, that's all.'

*

We discussed the short, brilliantly written essays by Alfred Polgar which often appeared in the *Prager Tagblatt*.

Kafka said, 'His sentences are so polished and pleasing that one looks on the reading of Alfred Polgar[41] as a welcome social diversion and hardly notices that one is being influenced and educated. The velvet glove of the form conceals the strong intrepid will which is the content. Polgar is a minor but effective Maccabee in the land of the Philistines.'

*

Franz Kafka said as he returned a book of poems by Francis Jammes:[42]

'He is so touchingly simple, so happy and strong. For him, his life is not an event between two nights. He knows nothing of darkness. He and his whole world nestle safely in God's almighty hand. Like a child, he lisps to the good God as to any member of the family. And so he does not grow old.'

*

Lydia Holzner gave me a Chinese novel, *The Three Leaps of Wanglun*, by Alfred Döblin. I showed it to Franz Kafka, who said:

'He has a great name among the modern German novelists. Apart from this book, his first, I only know some short stories and a strange novel about love, *The Black Curtain*. Döblin leaves me with the impression that he looks on the external world as something quite incomplete, to which he must give the final creative touches by his writing. That is only my impression. But if you read him attentively, you will soon notice the same thing.'[43]

*

Because of Kafka's comments, I read Alfred Döblin's first novel, *The Black Curtain, a novel of words and accidents*.

When I spoke to him about it, he said:

'I do not understand the book. Accident is the name one gives to the coincidence of events, of which one does not know the causation. But there is no world without causation. Therefore in the world there are no accidents, but only here . . .' Kafka touched his forehead with his left hand. 'Accidents only exist in our heads, in our limited perceptions. They are the reflection of the limits of our knowledge. The struggle against chance is always a struggle against ourselves, which we can never entirely win. But the book says nothing of all this.'

'So you are disappointed in Döblin?'

'As a matter of fact, I am only disappointed in myself. I expected from him something different from what he perhaps wished to give. But the stubbornness of my expectation blinded me so that I skipped pages and sentences and finally the whole book. So I can say nothing about the book. I am a very bad reader.'

*

Franz Kafka saw me with a book of Alfred Döblin's, *Murder of a Buttercup*.[44]

He said, 'How strange it sounds, when one takes a perfectly

ordinary idea from the world of a carnivorous culture and couples it with some frail botanical name.'

*

In three successive Sunday editions, the *Prager Presse* published an article, *The Great Literary Bestiary*, by Franz Blei. The author described a widely assorted number of writers and poets in the shape of fishes, birds, moles, hares, and so on. He said of Kafka amongst other things that he was a peculiar bird which fed on bitter roots.

I questioned Kafka about Franz Blei.

'He has been an old and close friend of Max Brod's for many years,' he said, smiling. 'Blei is enormously clever and witty. He is always so amusing when we meet. World literature parades past our table in its underpants. Franz Blei is much cleverer, and greater, than what he writes. That is natural, because his writing is only recorded conversation. The path from the head to the pen is much longer and harder than from the head to the tongue. Much is lost on the way. Franz Blei is an oriental storyteller who has lost his way to Germany.'[45]

*

Seeing me with a book of poems by Johannes R. Becher, he remarked:

'I do not understand these poems. They are so filled with noise and verbal uproar, that one cannot get away from oneself. Instead of bridges, the words form high unscalable walls. One is continually offended by the form, so that one can never penetrate to the content. The words never condense into language. They are a shriek and nothing more.'

*

Kafka showed me two pamphlets which lay on his desk before him. One was published by the National Association of Czechoslovak Legionaries and was addressed to the nation. The other pamphlet, which bore the signature of the 'Left

Fraction of the Czechs Social Democratic Party', summoned 'the working class to a mighty May Day demonstration'.

Kafka asked me: 'What do you think of them?'

I was silent and embarrassed, because I didn't know what I ought to say about the two pamphlets.

Kafka, who understood the reason for my embarrassment, without waiting for me to answer declared: 'The two pamphlets, which come from two opposing camps, have one thing in common. They are directed to completely unreal addresses. The nation, and the working class, are only abstract generalizations, dogmatic concepts, nebulous entities which can be apprehended only by a verbal manœuvre. Both concepts are real only as verbal constructions. Their existence is rooted in language, in its internal world, but not in the external world of men. The only reality is the concretely real human being, our neighbour, whom God puts in our path and to whose actions we are directly exposed.'

To this I remarked: 'Just as, for instance, the stoker is put in the path of the young Karl Rossmann.'

'Yes,' said Kafka. 'Like every concrete human being, he was a messenger from the outer world. Abstractions are only caricatures of one's own passions, ghosts from the dungeons of the world within.'

*

I was given two books by G. K. Chesterton, *Orthodoxy* and *The Man who was Thursday*.

Kafka said, 'He is so gay, that one might almost believe he had found God.'

'So for you laughter is a sign of religious feeling?'

'Not always. But in such a godless time one must be gay. It is a duty. The ship's orchestra played to the end on the sinking *Titanic*. In that way one saps the foundations of despair.'

'Yet a forced gaiety is much sadder than an openly acknowledged sorrow.'

'Quite true. Yet sorrow has no prospects. And all that matters is prospects, hope, going forward. There is danger only in the narrow, restricted moment. Behind it lies the abyss. If one overcomes it, everything is different. Only the moment counts. It determines life.'

*

We spoke about Baudelaire.

'Poetry is disease,' said Kafka. 'Yet one does not get well by suppressing the fever. On the contrary! Its heat purifies and illuminates.'

*

I lent Kafka the Czech translation of *Reminiscences of Leo Nikolaievich Tolstoy*, by Maxim Gorki.

Kafka said, 'It is remarkable how Gorki draws a man's character, without pronouncing any judgement. I should very much like one day to read his notes on Lenin.'

'Has Gorki published his reminiscences of Lenin?'

'No, not yet. But I assume that one day he certainly will. Lenin is a friend of Gorki's. But Maxim Gorki sees and experiences everything only through his pen. One realizes that from these notes on Tolstoy. The pen is not an instrument but an organ of the writer's.'

*

I quoted, from Grusemann's book on the author of *The Possessed*, the sentence: 'Dostoievsky is a fairy story drenched in blood.'[46]

Franz Kafka said in reply, 'There are no bloodless fairy stories. Every fairy story comes from the depths of blood and fear. In this all fairy stories are alike. Only the surface differs. Northern fairy stories lack the exuberant fauna of the imagination in the fairy stories of the African Negro, but the core, the depth of longing, is the same.'

... Some time later he recommended me to read Frobenius's collection of African folk-tales and fairy stories.[47]

*

Heinrich Heine.

Kafka: 'An unhappy man. The Germans reproached and still reproach him for being a Jew, and nevertheless he is a German, what is more a little German, who is in conflict with Jewry. That is what is so typically Jewish about him.'

*

Before and during the First World War, my parents subscribed to a large number of German and Czech newspapers and periodicals. Among them was the *Wiener Kronen-Zeitung*, a small cheap gossip-sheet, whose cover always consisted of reproductions of smart pen-and-ink drawings which I found fascinating.

They portrayed Archdukes, public houses going up in flames, imperial parades, air attacks by the then recently invented Zeppelins, Cossacks falling from their horses, Scottish bagpipes, scenes of murder and larceny, feats of life-saving in burning houses by men in smartly creased trousers and with turned-up moustaches, policemen with revolvers and drawn sabres, prize-winning dogs and horses, ladies in feather boas and hats like well-filled fruit baskets and many, many other sensational images which disclosed the hidden face of the age.

I collected the covers of the *Kronen-Zeitung* which interested me most and in the summer of 1918 had them bound together in a book with brightly marbled covers which I placed proudly in my bookshelf. Some three years later, Kafka said in the course of conversation, with reference to some modern poet whose name I don't remember, that the tone of his poetry was determined by the altar pieces of his youth. I said, laughing: 'My altar pieces come from the *Kronen-Zeitung*.'

At our next meeting, I showed Kafka my bound volume of covers. Kafka turned the pages over with interest, gazed with pleasure at the heaps of fruit and flowers on the ladies' hats, lingered a little longer over the scenes of the Russian Revolution and shook his head in exaggerated disgust – 'Ugh, how horrid!' – at the sight of a mutilated corpse on a Viennese prostitute's bed.

I said: 'It's a pictorial fruit salad – as colourful and contradictory as life itself.'

But Kafka shook his head in disagreement: 'No, that's not right. The pictures conceal more than they reveal. They don't penetrate into the depths, in which all contradictions meet each other. Events are recorded here simply as a means of making money. In this respect the pictures in the *Kreuz-Zeitung* are more realistic than, but therefore inferior to, the popular woodcuts in the broadsheets of the old fairs. At least they had a little imagination, which allowed one to reach beyond oneself. These drawings don't do anything like that. They break the wings of the imagination. That's perfectly natural. The more the technique of painting improves, the weaker our eyes get. The instrument damages the organs. It's the same in optics, in acoustics, in transport. As a result of the war, America has come to Europe. The continents have shrunk together. A spark carries a man's voice round the world in an instant. We no longer live in a space cut to human size but on a small lost star surrounded by millions of larger and smaller worlds. Solar space looms up like an act of vengeance. In its abysses we lose more and more of our freedom of movement day by day. I believe that it can't last much longer and we shall require special movement papers in order to leave our own front door. The world is changing into a ghetto.' I said cautiously: 'Isn't what you're saying rather exaggerated?' But Kafka shook his head. 'No, not in the least! I see it here already at the Insurance Institution. The world is opening out but we are driven into narrow defiles of paper. The only certainty is the chair one sits on. We live in straight lines, yet every man is in fact a labyrinth. Writing desks are beds of Procrustes. Yet we are not antique heroes. So, despite our pain, all we are is tragic comedians.'

*

'Most men are not wicked,' said Franz Kafka, talking of Leonhard Frank's book *Man is Good*.[48] 'Men become bad and guilty because they speak and act without foreseeing the results of their words and their deeds. They are sleepwalkers, not evildoers.'

*

Kafka was in very good spirits.

'You sparkle today,' I said.

Kafka smiled.

'It is only a borrowed light. The reflection of a friendly word. A very good friend, Ludwig Hardt, is in Prague.'49

'Is that the reciter, who is to appear in the Corn Exchange?'

'Yes, that is Ludwig Hardt. Do you know him?'

'No, I don't know him. I only saw the advertisement in the newspaper. What is more, recitations don't interest me.'

'Ludwig Hardt must interest you. He is not a pretentious virtuoso. Ludwig Hardt is a servant of the word. He revives and brings to life poems that are buried under the dust of convention. He is a great man.'

'How did you come to know him?'

'I met him through Max ten years ago. On our very first meeting I listened to him for the entire evening. He is an enchanting man. So free, untroubled, vigorous. He comes from somewhere in the north, is a typical Jew, and yet he is a stranger nowhere. The first moment I saw him I felt that I should go on knowing him for a long long time. He is a magician.'

'In what sense a magician?'

'I don't know. But he can stimulate a powerful feeling of freedom. That is why he is a magician. Anyhow we will attend his performance together. I will get the tickets.'

Before Hardt's recital we met the poet Rudolf Fuchs50 on the steps of the Corn Exchange. We stood with him at the front near the entrance. Kafka attended carefully to the artist, but his look was one of inner oppression. I saw that he had great difficulty in keeping his attention to the programme.

'Are you not feeling well?' I asked in the interval, when Fuchs had left us for a moment.

Kafka raised his eyebrows.

'Do I look strange? Is there anything noticeable?'

'No. Only that you seem so peculiar.'

Kafka smiled with narrow, tight-pressed lips.

'It would be very easy to explain myself by being physically unwell. Unfortunately it is nothing of the kind. I feel only a deadly tiredness and emptiness, which always set in whenever something delights me. Probably I have no imagination. Things melt away. Only my grey, hopeless prison-cell remains.'

I did not fully understand his words, but the return of Rudolf Fuchs prevented any questions. After the recital I said good night to Kafka, who with Fuchs, Weltsch, Frau Brod, and others waited for Hardt.

The next day I called on Franz Kafka in his office. He was somewhat taciturn and engaged in no discussion of our evening in the Corn Exchange. Only when I remarked that I knew Rudolf Fuchs's book of poems *Caravan* and his translation of the hymns of Otokar Březina, did he become a little livelier and say:

'Rudolf Fuchs reads with such profound devotion, that he gives not only every good book but every sincere word of a poet a value far above his own humble soul. Therefore he is such a good translator and writes so little himself. His *Caravan* distributes the products of foreign markets. He is a servant of the word.'

We never spoke about Ludwig Hardt again.

*

My father gave me for my birthday the poems of Georg Trakl. Franz Kafka told me that Trakl committed suicide by taking poison, to escape the horrors of the war.

'A deserter to Death,' I said.

'He had too much imagination,' said Kafka. 'So he could not endure the war, which arose above all from a monstrous lack of imagination.'

*

I was ill for ten days, stayed in bed, and did not go to school.

My father brought me warm greetings from Kafka and a brightly coloured volume in the *Insel-Bücherei*: Arthur Schopenhauer, *On Writing and Style*.

A few days after recovering I visited the Workmen's Accident Insurance Institution. Kafka was in very good spirits. When I told him that I felt much better after my illness, a charming smile appeared on his face.

'That is quite natural,' he said. 'You have overcome a meeting with death. That gives one strength.'

'All one's life is only a journey towards death,' I said.

Franz Kafka looked at me gravely for a moment, then lowered his glance to his desk.

'For healthy people, life is only an unconscious and unavowed flight from the consciousness that one day one must die. Illness is always a warning and a trial of strength. And so illness, pain, suffering are the most important sources of religious feeling.'

'In what sense?' I asked.

Kafka smiled.

'In a Jewish sense. I am bound to my family and my race. They outlive the individual. But that also is only an attempted flight from the knowledge of death. It is only a wish. And by such means one gains no knowledge. On the contrary – by such a wish the little, terribly egoistic "I" prefers itself to the truth-seeking soul.'

*

'What are you reading?' asked Kafka.

'*Tashkent, the Bountiful City*, by . . .'[51]

He did not allow me to finish the sentence.

'It is wonderful. I read it one afternoon a short time ago.'

'It seems to me that the book is more of a document than a work of art,' I said.

'All true art is a document, a statement of evidence,' said Franz Kafka gravely. 'A people with children like those in the book, a people like that can never go under.'

'Perhaps it does not depend on individuals.'

'On the contrary! The species of matter is determined by the number of electrons in the atom. The level of the masses depends on the consciousness of individuals.'

*

When I entered his office, Kafka was busy turning out his desk. On the narrow side to the right, where a chair stood ready for any visitor who might arrive, lay a pile of books, newspapers and office memoranda. Kafka waved to me across the desk.

'Greetings from my paper dungeon!'

I sat in the visitor's chair and said:

'That's a real forest of documents. You've completely disappeared in it.' I heard Kafka's brief laugh, then immediately he said: 'Then everything is in order. What is written illuminates the world. But the writer disappears into darkness. So away with it!'

He pulled out the middle drawer, opened the side compartments, and began to stuff the pile of books and papers into the desk.

I wanted to help him. But when I handed him one of the files he shook his head vigorously.

'Leave it! Quite by accident we might be unlucky enough to put things in order. Then I'd be in trouble. I might lose the excuse, which is extremely important to every conscientious official, that I had been unable to perform my appointed task, not through lack of professional competence, but because of the infernal disorder of my desk. That would be a terrible revelation, which I must avoid at all costs. Therefore I must carefully preserve the disorder of my desk.'

As a proof, he slammed the middle drawer shut with a violent jerk, and said, in an exaggeratedly sinister and conspiratorial voice: 'My complaints about the disorder in the office, and especially around myself, are only a trick, by which I try to hide the insecurity of my existence from the accusing and inquisitive gaze of the outside world. In reality, I only manage to live because of the disorder, from which I steal the last remnant of personal freedom.'

*

I accompanied Kafka from the office to his home. It was a cold autumn day, swept by rain and wind.

Kafka said to me on the steps that he could not talk in the open air in such weather.

'That doesn't matter,' I said. 'We shall understand each other all the same.'

Nevertheless as we emerged from the entrance of the Workmen's Accident Insurance Institution, Kafka stooped, shook himself vigorously, crossed himself with a great Roman cross, and for me all understanding ceased.

Kafka smiled at my astonished face, went back into the building, and said:

'I was speaking Czech – *sakramentská velka zimá!* My stooping indicated the force which overpowered me, shivering is the traditional way of expressing cold, and the Cross, that precisely is the sacrament.'

For some unknown reason, his gaiety offended me, and so I said:

'The sign of the Cross is not a sacrament.'

He laid his hand on my shoulder.

'Not only every sign, but even the merest gesture, is holy if it is filled with faith.'

*

I told Kafka about the hunger and misery of the lace workers and toymakers in the Erzgebrige, which I had crossed in 1919 with my brother Hans, a railway official in Obergeorgenthal (Czech: Horní Jiretín) near Brüx. I ended my account with the words: 'Trade and industry, the health services, food supplies – nothing, nothing works properly. The world is in ruins.' But Kafka did not agree. He drew his underlip in, chewed it for a few seconds, then said very firmly: 'That is not true. If everything were in ruins, we should already have reached a point of departure towards new possibilities of development. But as yet we have not gone so far. The way that leads out of it has disappeared. So also have all the perspectives of the future which we previously shared. We are going through a hopeless decline. One look out of the window will show the world to you. Where are the people going? What do they want? We no longer recognize the metaphysical order of things. In spite of all the noise, everyone is dumb and isolated within himself. The interrelation of objective and personal values doesn't function any more. We live not in a ruined but a bewildered world. Everything creaks and rattles like the rigging of an unseaworthy sailing ship. The misery which you and your brother saw is only the surface expression of a much deeper distress.'

Kafka looked me in the eyes as if to ask me anxiously: 'Do you understand me? Am I confusing you?' So I made haste to reply at least with a question: 'Do you mean the injustice of society?'

But Kafka's face became hard and impenetrable.

He said: 'I mean the fall from justice. We all have a hand in it. We sense it. Some are even conscious of it. But no one will admit that we live in a state of evil. Therefore we find ways of escape. We talk about social, spiritual, national and who knows what other kinds of injustice, only in order to excuse one single fault, which is our own fault. For what is the word *injustice*? It is a contraction of the expression *our justice*. A justice which only applies to myself is a rule of violence, an injustice. The expression, social injustice, is only one of many camouflage operations.'

I shook my head. 'No. I can't agree with that. I saw the misery in the Erzgebrige. The factories are – '

Kafka interrupted me. 'The factories are merely organizations for increasing financial profit. In such a matter, we all have a merely subordinate function. Man is today only an old-fashioned instrument of economic growth, a hangover from history, whose economically inadequate skills will soon be displaced by frictionless thinking machines.'

I sighed disdainfully: 'Oh yes, that's a favourite Utopia of H. G. Wells.'

'No,' said Kafka in a hard voice, 'that's no Utopia, but only the future which already looms before us.'

*

Kafka was a convinced adherent of Zionism. We first discussed this subject in the spring of 1920, when I had returned to Prague after a short stay in the country.

At that time I called on Franz Kafka in the office on the Pořič. He was in good spirits, talkative and, it seemed to me, genuinely pleased by an unexpected visit.

'I thought you were far away, and here you are on my doorstep. Weren't you happy in Chlumetz?'

'Oh yes, but . . .'

'But here it's better,' concluded Kafka, smiling.

'You know – home is home. Elsewhere things are quite different.'

'Home is always different,' said Franz Kafka, with dream-veiled eyes. 'The old home is always new, if one lives consciously, with a sharp awareness of one's relations and duties to others. Men are only free in this way, through their relations to others. And that is the greatest thing in life.'

'Life without freedom is impossible,' I declared.

Franz Kafka looked at me, as if to say, 'Gently, gently,' smiled sadly and said:

'That sounds so convincing that we almost believe it. In fact, things are more difficult. Freedom is life. Lack of liberty is death. But death is just as much a reality as life. And that is precisely the difficulty: that we are exposed to both – to life as well as death.'

'Then it follows that you regard a lack of national independence as a mark of death. The Czech of 1913 is less alive and therefore worse than the Czech of 1920.'

'I did not mean that,' Kafka protested. 'One cannot draw such a sharp distinction between the Czech of 1913 and the Czech of 1920. The Czechs of today have much greater possibilities. Therefore they may be better – if one can speak in such terms.'

'I don't quite understand.'

'I can't make it any clearer and in any case I cannot perhaps express myself any better on such a subject, because I am a Jew.'

'Why not, what has that to do with it?'

'We were talking about the Czechs in 1913 and 1920. To a certain extent that is an historical problem, and so – if I may say so – it immediately brings into question one of the disabilities of the Jews today.'

I must have made a very stupid face, for – to judge by Kafka's voice and attitude – he was more concerned at the moment about my understanding than about the matter under discussion. Leaning forward, he spoke softly, yet clearly and distinctly:

'The Jews today are no longer satisfied with history, with an heroic home in time. They yearn for a modest ordinary home in space. More and more young Jews are returning to Palestine. That is a return to oneself, to one's roots, to growth. The national home in Palestine is for the Jews a necessary goal. On the other hand, for the Czechs, Czechoslovakia is a point of departure.'

'A kind of aerodrome?'

Franz Kafka inclined his head towards his left shoulder.

'Do you think they will ever take off? It seems to me as if I saw in them too great a departure from their foundations, from their own sources of strength. I have never heard of a young eagle learning to make a real eagle's flight by continually and obstinately studying the manœuvres of a portly carp.'

*

With Kafka beside the Moldau as far as the National Theatre. From there to the Graben and then to the left by the Bergmann – and the Eisenstrasse back to the Altstädter Ring. On the way we met Franz P., the star pupil and 'know-all' with whom I had been in school for several years. Now we passed each other with a hasty greeting. As we walked on I told Kafka how we – that is, the gang of boys to which I once belonged – could not stand P. and ostracized him at every opportunity. Finally I said: 'That's a long time ago now. In the end I was reconciled to P. and even took his side against the other boys.'

'With what success?' asked Kafka dryly.

'I think, considerable,' I replied. 'At first there were blows and bloody noses on both sides, but that didn't last for long. The boys saw they couldn't beat P. and me up so easily any more, so they gave up hostilities.'

'Attack and defence cancelled each other out,' said Kafka.

I nodded. 'Yes, they left us alone.'

Kafka gave a gentle, chuckling laugh and said: 'That was an important victory. To impose an armistice on the enemy is the greatest victory one can achieve. But the final destruction of evil? One can't expect that. That's a lunatic dream by which evil is not weakened but – quite the contrary – is strengthened and its effect accelerated, because one overlooks its real nature and distorts reality into an illusion founded on one's own misleading wishes.' We stood outside the door of Kafka's house. He threw his head back, let his eyes roam slowly across the front of the house, then asked, without looking at me: 'Do you know how many steps there are up to my room?'

'I have no idea.'

Kafka looked away from me. 'Neither have I; I've never counted them. I couldn't risk it. If I knew the exact number of steps, perhaps, with my shortness of breath, I'd probably be frightened at every single one of them.' He smiled. 'It's better to face difficulties as one faces oneself, and only look at them minute by minute.' Kafka looked me gravely in the face. After a few seconds he said, again averting his glance: 'The dream of destroying evil is only a reflection of the sense of despair which comes from loss of faith.'

*

In the first Czechoslovak Republic, under the leadership of T. G. Masaryk, after the first general elections to the Parliament and Senate, there followed such a violent propaganda battle between all the parties that no one could remain unaffected by it. It even entered into our conversations, as Kafka's friend for many years, Max Brod, was a candidate for the Zionist Party of the Czechoslovak Republic. This caused a certain sensation, because until then Brod had been well known as a critic, a novelist, and a philosopher of culture, but not as a practising politician. So his articles in the Zionist newspaper, *Self-Defence*, aroused great interest. My father, however, was of the opinion that Brod's party would hardly win the necessary number of votes in a single constituency. To a certain extent Kafka also shared this view.

He said: 'Brod and his political friends are convinced that the Zionist Party will certainly gain the necessary number of votes in the eastern Slovak town of Eperjes.'

'Is that your opinion also?'

'To be honest – no! Brod's belief that the conditions for a Zionist victory exist there is based on the fact that for a short time after the war Eperjes had its own Czechoslovak soviet government, which broke down primarily because it was not supported by the Jewish population of Eperjes. Max draws the conclusion that there are possibilities of development for the Zionists. But that's quite false. The Jews of Eperjes are, like everyone else in the world, only a microcosm of the other parties. They have no modern, national consciousness but only an ancient racialism. Objectively, they attach themselves for the most part to the legally dominant authority. So the Jews of Eperjes did not support the hastily improvised soviet government. Their passivity was rooted, not in Jewish nationalism, but in Jewish need of something to prop them up. I tried to persuade Max Brod of this. But he didn't understand. He does not understand that Jewish nationalism, as expressed in Zionism, is only a form of defence. That's why the Zionists' party newspaper in Prague is called *Self-Defence*. Jewish nationalism is like a caravan which in the cold of a desert night is forced by outside pressures to form a powerful lager. The caravan doesn't want to win a victory. It only wants to reach some secure and peaceful homeland of its own which will give the men and women of the caravan the possibility of a freely developing human existence. The Jewish longing for a homeland is not an aggressive nationalism wdich – being fundamentally homeless both subjectively and objectively – grasps ferociously at foreign homesteads, because – again, fundamentally speaking – it is incapable of making the desert bloom again.'

'Are you thinking of the Germans?'

Kafka was silent; he coughed, put his hand to his mouth, and said wearily: 'I am thinking of the lust for booty of all those groups of people who, by laying waste the word, do not enlarge their own dominions but only restrict their own humanity. Zionism, by comparison, is only a painful passage back to its own human laws.'

*

In a large corner house on the Bergstein I was looking for the meeting-room of the Jewish Working Men's Association, the *Poale Zion*.[52] When I spoke to a group of people in the dark courtyard, instead of the information I asked for, I received several blows in the face, so that I took to flight.

The caretaker, whom I fetched, of course found no one left in the courtyard. In a bad temper, he inquired:

'But what do you want from these Jews? After all, you are not a Jew.'

I shook my head.

'No, I am not a Jew.'

'There you are,' said the guardian of the law triumphantly. 'There you have it! What have you to do with that rabble? Thank your stars you only got a couple of punches on the nose, and go back home. Decent people don't mix with Jews.'

*

A few days later I told Kafka about my misadventure.

'Anti-semitism increases with Zionism,' he said. 'The self-determination of the Jews is felt as a denial of their environment. As a result inferiority complexes are created which easily come to a head in outbursts of hatred. Of course, in the long run nothing is gained. But that is the root of men's guilt, that they prefer the evil which lies so temptingly close at hand to the moral values which seem so difficult to attain.'

'Perhaps men cannot act otherwise,' I said.

Kafka shook his head vigorously.

'No. Men can act otherwise. The Fall is the proof of their freedom.'

*

Franz Kafka remarked in the course of a conversation about an anthology of Jewish stories from Eastern Europe:53

'Perez, Asch, and all the other Eastern European Jewish writers always write stories which are in fact folk-stories. And that is quite right. Jewry is not merely a question of faith, it is above all a question of the practice of a way of life in a community conditioned by faith.'

*

My friend Leo Lederer gave me an illustrated monograph on Michelangelo.

I showed the book to Franz Kafka, and for a long time he studied the picture of the seated Moses.

'That is not a leader,' he said. 'He is a judge, a stern judge. In the end men can only lead by means of harsh, inexorable judgement.'

*

I went to the swimming pool when very hot. The result was a slight inflammation of the lungs.

When I could go out again, I visited Kafka in the Insurance Institution. 'You are undisciplined,' he said reproachfully after we had exchanged greetings. 'Your illness was a warning. You must take better care of yourself. Good health is not a personal possession, to do what one likes with. It is property on loan, a grace. Most people do not realize this. So they have no hygienic economy.'

'They dive into the water when overheated,' I said with a smile. Kafka nodded. 'Yes, they squander themselves. And so they are given the warning sign of illness. Usually, it's people's own fault. But they do not recognize it. On the contrary; it's life that's to blame. And so men run to the doctor – barristers of health – to bring an action against life for its wickedness.

But illness isn't wickedness, it's a warning sign, an aid to living.'

I looked at the ground in confusion.

'It's strange,' I answered in embarrassment, 'that you of all people who have had so much to do with illness, should – I can only put it this way – talk of it as if it were a friend.'

'That's not strange at all,' cried Kafka, with a vigorous shake of the head. 'It's perfectly natural. I am a proud and over-bearing person; I will not accept the full extent of the hardness of life. I am the only son of fairly prosperous parents and believe that life is something which comes naturally to one. And so by illness I am perpetually reminded of the full extent of my frailty and therewith of the miracle of life.'

'So illness is therefore a grace?'

'Yes. It gives us the possibility of protecting ourselves.'

*

Telling me about his journeys in Germany and France, he said of Max Brod:

'These travels strengthened our friendship. That is only natural. In foreign surroundings, the native and familiar becomes clearer and more distinct to us. That – I think – is the source of Jewish jokes about Jews. We see each other better than other people, because we are together on a journey.'

*

A walk on the quay.

I asked the meaning of the word 'Diaspora'. Kafka said it was the Greek expression for the dispersion of the Jewish people. The Hebrew word is 'Galut'.

He said, 'The Jewish people is scattered, as a seed is scattered. As a seed of corn absorbs matter from its surroundings, stores it up, and achieves further growth, so the destiny of the Jews is to absorb the potentialities of mankind, purify them, and give them a higher development. Moses is still a reality. As Abiram and Dathan opposed Moses with the words '*Lo naale!* We will not go up!' so the world opposes him with the cry of anti-semitism. In order not to rise to the human condition, men sink into the dark depths of the zoological doctrine of race. They beat the Jews, and murder humanity.'

*

'Jews and Germans have much in common,' said Kafka, in a conversation about Dr Karel Kramář.[54] 'They are energetic, able, industrious, and thoroughly detested by everyone else. Jews and Germans are outcasts.'

'Perhaps they are hated for the very qualities you mention,' I said.

But Kafka shook his head.

'Oh, no! There is a much deeper reason. In the end, it is a religious reason. In the case of the Jews, this is clear. In the case of the Germans, it is not so apparent, because their temple has not yet been destroyed. But that will come.'

'What do you mean?' I said in bewilderment. 'After all, the Germans are not a theocracy. They have no national God in a temple of his own.'

'So most people think, but in fact it is not so,' said Kafka. 'The Germans have the God, who made the iron grow. His temple is the Prussian General Staff.'

We laughed. Franz Kafka, however, declared that he was perfectly serious and only laughed because I did. His laughter was only an infection.

*

I accompanied Kafka from the Accident Insurance Institution to his house. This time, however, we did not go by the Zeltnerstrasse but across the Graben. On the way we talked about a new book of stories by a successful Austrian writer of fantastic novels and tales.

'He has an immense talent for invention,' I said in his praise. But Kafka only curled his lip slightly and said: 'Invention is easier than discovery. To present reality in all its detailed, and if possible in its most comprehensive, diversity is certainly the hardest task there is. The faces one sees every day rush by one like a mysterious army of insects.'

For a moment he abstractedly contemplated the traffic at the road junction in the middle of the Wenzelsplatz, where we were standing at the corner of the Bruckels- and the Obstgasse.

'What are all these meetings about? Every face is a fortress tower. Yet nothing vanishes so rapidly as a human face.'

I smiled: 'Flies and fleas are hard to catch.'

'Yes: come along,' said Kafka, turned around and with long strides hurried along the Gasse Am Bruckel.

*

On the Jungmannplatz, we visited the Franciscan Church of the *Virgin in the Snows*, which has the highest nave in Prague. Kafka was interested in its name. Fortunately, I was able to explain to him the origin of the church's strange name, because I sometimes used to listen to performances of old Czech church music there and had taken the opportunity to learn about the church.

According to an ancient legend, there lived in Rome a rich and very pious citizen, who in a dream was commissioned by the Mother of God to build a church dedicated to her on the spot where snow fell on the following day. This occurred towards the end of midsummer A.D. 352. Thus it was a perfectly absurd dream, yet it proved true, because the next day in Rome the Esquiline Hill was covered with snow. The Roman citizen, whose name I have forgotten, accordingly built the first church of the *Virgin in the Snows*. His dream, which led to the foundation of the church in Rome, is portrayed on the high altar-piece of Prague's Franciscan church of the *Virgin in the Snows*. I showed it to Kafka and ended my story by saying: 'The name of the church derives from this miraculous dream.' Kafka replied: 'I never knew that. I only know the story of the later chroniclers. According to them, in the fifteenth century this church was a meeting place of the most extreme Hussites.'

We walked on.

For a moment there flickered on Kafka's face the ghost of a

smile, then immediately his mouth became tight-lipped and he said: 'Miracles and violence are simply the two extremes of a lack of faith. Men waste their lives in passive expectation of some miraculous directive, which never comes, precisely because our ears are closed to it by exaggerated expectations; or, filled with impatience, they cast aside all expectations and drown their whole lives in a criminal orgy of fire and blood. Both ways are wrong.'

'What is right?' I asked.

'This,' said Kafka without hesitation and pointed to an old woman kneeling in a lady chapel near the way out. 'Prayer.'

He put his hand under my arm and with a gentle pressure led me to the church door. When we reached the forecourt, he said: 'Prayer, art and scientific research are three different flames that leap up from the same hearth. Man wants to cross the frontier of the possible achievements that lie open to him at any given moment, to reach beyond the limitations of his own small self. Art and prayer are only hands outstretched in the dark. People beg to give themselves away.'

'And science?'

'It is the same begging hand as prayer. Man throws himself into the dark rainbow which spans dying and living, in order to offer existence a home in the cradle of his little ego. That is what science, art and prayer all do. So that to sink into oneself is not to fall into the unconscious, but to raise what is only dimly divined into the bright surface of consciousness.'

*

We were standing – Kafka, my father and myself – at the window of the Workmen's Accident Insurance Institution. In the street, a club in gay peasants' costume was marching by with flags and a brass band. I said: 'What are these people doing in the ancient uniforms of feudal serfdom. That was all over long ago.'

'As you see, it still lives,' said my father. 'It's an old popular tradition.'

Kafka laughed: 'So are all forms of idolatry.'

'You mean nationalism?' I asked.

'Yes,' said Kafka. 'That also is a substitute for religion. The people marching past us here are carrying their own idols. From the outside, they look quite small and inoffensive. During jolly hours of beer drinking, people have pasted them together out of their own fears and their own will to achieve significance. Nevertheless, all of us will find that their totem poles have turned into crucifixes, for there are no idols more devouring than these filthy goblins made out of beer, spittle and newsprint.'

*

Franz Kafka told me that the Prague Jewish poet Oskar Baum had as a small boy attended the German primary school. On the way home there were frequently fights between the German and the Czech pupils. In one of these scuffles, Oskar Baum was hit over the eyes with a wooden pencil-box so hard, that the retina came away from the base of the eyeball, and Oskar Baum lost his sight.

'The Jew Oskar Baum lost his eyesight as a German,' said Franz Kafka. 'As something in fact which he never was, and which he was never accepted as being. Perhaps Oskar is merely a melancholy symbol of the so-called German Jews in Prague.'

*

We spoke about the relations of the Germans and the Czechs. I said that to publish a Czech history in German would make for better understanding between the two nations.

Kafka, however, dismissed this with a resigned wave of the hand.

'It would be pointless,' he said. 'Who would read it? Only Czechs and Jews. Certainly not the Germans, because they do not wish to comprehend, understand, read. They only wish to possess and to rule, and for that understanding is usually only a hindrance. One oppresses one's neighbour much better when one doesn't know him. The pangs of conscience disappear. For that reason, no one knows the history of the Jews.'

I protested, 'That isn't true. Even in the first form of the primary school they teach Scripture, that is to say, a part of the history of the Jewish people.'

Kafka smiled bitterly.

'Just so! The history of the Jews is given the appearance of a fairy tale, which men can dismiss, together with their childhood, into the pit of oblivion.'

*

I was saying goodbye to my friend Leo Lederer on the Square of the Republic when Franz Kafka unexpectedly approached me.

'I followed you all the way from Teschnov,' he said after the usual words of greeting. 'You were quite lost in your conversation.'

'Leo was explaining Taylorism to me, and the division of labour in industry.'

'It is a terrible subject.'

'You are thinking of the enslavement of mankind?'

'It is much worse than that. Such a violent outrage can only end in enslavement to evil. It is inevitable. Time, the noblest and most essential element in all creative work, is conscripted into the net of corrupt business interests. Thereby not only creative work, but man himself, who is its essential part, is polluted and humiliated. A Taylorized life is a terrible curse which will give rise only to hunger and misery instead of the intended wealth and profit. It is an advance . . .'

'Towards the end of the world,' I completed his sentence.

Franz Kafka shook his head.

'If one could only say that with certainty. But it is by no means certain. So one can say nothing. One can only scream, stammer, choke. The conveyor belt of life carries one somewhere – but one doesn't know where. One is a thing, an object – rather than a living organism.'

Kafka suddenly stood still and stretched out his hand.

'Look! There, there! Can you see it?'

Out of a house in the Jakobsgasse, where we had arrived in the course of our discussion, ran a small dog looking like a ball of wool, which crossed our path and disappeared round the corner of the Tempelgasse.

'A pretty little dog,' I said.

'A dog?' asked Kafka suspiciously, and slowly began to move again.

'A small, young dog. Didn't you see it?'

'I saw. But was it a dog?'

'It was a little poodle.'

'A poodle? It could be a dog, but it could also be a sign. We Jews often make tragic mistakes.'

'It was only a dog,' I said.

'It would be a good thing if it was.' Kafka nodded. 'But the *only* is true only for him who uses it. What one person takes to be a bundle of rags, or a dog, is for another a sign.'

'Odradek,55 in your story *The Cares of the Father*,' I said.

Kafka did not respond to my words, and continued his former train of thought with a final sentence:

'There is always something unaccounted for.'

We walked in silence across the Teinhof. At the side door of the Teinkirche I said:

'Bloy writes that the tragic guilt of the Jews is that they did not recognize the Messiah.'

'Perhaps that is really so,' said Kafka. 'Perhaps they really did not recognize him. But what a cruel God it is who makes it possible for his creatures not to recognize him. After all, a father always makes himself known to his children, when they cannot think or speak properly. But this is not a subject for a conversation on the street. Besides, I've reached home.'

Kafka nodded his head towards his father's warehouse, stretched out his hand and said goodbye, and with rapid steps disappeared into the Kinsky Palace.

*

I had with me a review, published by the Salesians, which contained an account of a boy's town founded near Omaha in Nebraska in 1917 by an Irish priest, Father Flanagan. Kafka read the article and said:

'All our towns and monuments have been created by crazy children like that, who have found freedom in submission.'

*

A walk over the Charles Bridge, past the Kleinseitner tower, through the Sachsen alley to the Grossprioratsplatz. From there through the Prokopius alley to the Eiermarkt – today: Kleinseitner Marktplatz – up to the Bretislavgasse and over the wide Johannisberger steps to the Spornergasse. Then down to the Kleinseitner Ring to the tramway.

Kafka explained the statues on the bridge to me, pointed out various details and showed me ancient house-signs, gateways, window embrasures and lattice work. On the Charles Bridge he pointed with his outstretched right hand to a little sandstone angel holding its nose between its outstretched fingers behind a statue of the Virgin.

'It behaves,' said Kafka, 'as if Heaven stank. But for a heavenly being like an angel, everything earthly must in any case have a bad smell.'

'But the statue at whose feet the angel is cowering,' I said, 'is an image of the Mother of God.'

'Just so!' cried Kafka. 'Nothing is more earthly, but also nothing reaches further beyond the earth, than motherhood. Through the pain of birth a new glimmer of hope and with it a new possibility of happiness are implanted in our earthly dust.'

I said nothing.

As we passed by the Eiermarkt to the Schönborn palace, Kafka said: 'This is not a city. It is a fissure in the ocean bed of time, covered with the stony rubble of burned-out dreams and passions, through which we – as if in a diving bell – take a walk. It's interesting, but after a time one loses one's breath. Like all divers, one has to come to the surface, otherwise the blood bursts one's lungs. I have lived here a long time. I had to go away. It was too much.'

'Yes,' I said, 'the roads to the Inner Town are not good. One has to cross ancient stone bridges and then through a maze of tortuous alleys. There's no direct route.'

Kafka was silent for a few moments. Then he responded to my remark with a question, which he immediately answered himself.

He said: 'Is there a direct route anywhere at all for us? A direct route is only a dream, and that only leads to error.'

I looked at Kafka in bewilderment. What connection was there between dreams and the route from the Kleinseite to the Insurance Institution on the Pořič?

To hide my increasing bewilderment, I said aloud: 'Even by tram one doesn't make any direct progress. One has to change and usually there's a long wait before one gets a connection.'

Kafka, however, seemed not to hear me. He proceeded down the steep Spornergasse, his chin up, his hands buried in the pockets of his thin grey overcoat, with such rapid steps that I, who hardly came up to his shoulder, had to make a determined effort to keep up with him. Kafka, however, only seemed to become aware of my forced march when we were down on the Kleinstädter Ring.

He stood at the stop for the electric tram and said with an embarrassed smile: 'It looks as though I wanted to escape you. Didn't I go too fast?'

'It wasn't so bad,' I replied, and wiped my sweat-soaked collar with my handkerchief. 'One always walks faster when one goes downhill.'

But Kafka wouldn't agree.

'No, no! It's not just the fault of the hill. It's the steep declivity within me. I roll to rest like a ball. It's a weakness through which one loses one's balance.'

'It wasn't so bad,' I repeated, but he shook his head.

He looked over my head towards the entrance to the Thomasgasse. Then softly he went on talking. It was like a monologue spoken aloud.

'The quiet among these old houses is like a charge of dynamite which bursts all internal barriers. One's legs run down the hill and one's voice creates – literally – a mountain of images. The frontier between inner and outer vanishes. One marches through the streets as if through dark canals of time's dishwater. One listens to one's own voice and feels as if one were hearing something exceptionally clever and witty. But it's only a case of compulsive disguise for one's own personal loss of value. One, as it were, looks down on oneself with contempt. All that's lacking is for one to search one's pockets for a fountain pen and a writing pad in order to write an anonymous letter to oneself.'

From the Thomasgasse there now emerged a slowly moving tram. Kafka started, as if he had just woken up.

He said, 'There, this is our number. We can get on,' and smiling he put his hand under my arm.

*

Franz Kafka turned the pages of a book by Alfons Paquet, *The Spirit of the Russian Revolution*, which I had brought with me to his office.

'Would you like to read it?' I asked.

'No, thank you,' said Kafka, and handed me the book across his desk. 'At the moment I have no time. A pity. In Russia men are trying to construct an absolutely just world. It is a religious matter.'

'But Bolshevism is opposed to religion.'

'That is because it is itself a religion. These interventions, revolts, the blockade – what are they? They are little rehearsals for the great and cruel religious wars, which will sweep across the world.'

*

We met a large group of workmen who were marching with flags and banners to a meeting.

Kafka said, 'These people are so self-possessed, so self-confident and good-humoured. They rule the streets, and therefore think they rule the world. In fact, they are mistaken. Behind them already are the secretaries, officials, professional politicians, all the modern satraps for whom they are preparing the way to power.'

'You do not believe in the power of the masses?'

'It is before my eyes, this power of the masses, formless and apparently chaotic, which then seeks to be given a form and a discipline. At the end of every truly revolutionary development there appears a Napoleon Bonaparte.'

'You don't believe in a wider expansion of the Russian Revolution?'

Kafka was silent for a moment, then he said:

'As a flood spreads wider and wider, the water becomes shallower and dirtier. The Revolution evaporates, and leaves behind only the slime of a new bureaucracy. The chains of tormented mankind are made out of red tape.'

*

One did not have to have much particular insight to see that Kafka's life in the office was a torment to him. He often sat behind his large empty desk, bent and sunk into himself, his face greyish-yellow. But if one asked how he was, he always replied with forced gaiety: 'Thank you, I'm very well.'

This rebuff was a conscious lie, which was something which was totally out of Kafka's character; according both to my father, and to some of his colleagues whom I knew, in the whole of the Accident Insurance Institution there was not a more truthful or conscientious man than Kafka. According to my father, Kafka had said to him several times: 'Without truth, which everyone understands, and to which therefore everyone willingly subordinates himself, all authority is naked force, a cage which sooner or later falls to pieces under the pressure of the need for truth.'

My father and his colleagues saw in Kafka's love of truth the expression of a strongly developed ethical will; but in fact it was – according to Kafka's own words – something quite different.

I came to know this in the following way.

At the time of my first visits to Kafka, I often reacted to his words with the astonished question: 'Is that really true?' At first Kafka would only reply with a brief word. When I had known him for longer, and still expressed my astonishment with my stereotyped question, he once said to me: 'Please don't ask that question any more. That single sentence strips me naked in my own eyes. I see my own incapacity. Lying is an act and – like every other act – demands all a man's skill. One must give up everything to it, one must first believe in the lie oneself, because only then can one convince other people. Lying demands the heat of passion. For that reason, it reveals more than it conceals. I am not capable of that. So for me there is only one hiding-place – the truth.'

A soft, whispering elfin laugh came from his half-open lips. I laughed with him. But mine was only a feeble laugh of embarrassment. For fundamentally I was ashamed of myself, of how superficially I used words in my meetings with Kafka. I was all the more ashamed because shortly before Kafka had said to me: 'Language clothes what is indestructible in us, a garment which survivies us.'

I no longer know how I stammered my way out of my shameful confusion, I only know that from then on I took greater care of what I was saying. Not only in conversation with Kafka, but in my contacts with everyone. That heightened my powers of perception. I learned to observe and to listen better. Thereby my life became deeper and more complicated but without becoming more cold and detached. On the contrary; the almost infinite complexity of things and people, which never failed to astonish me, made my existence richer and more meaningful. I was carried through time on a wave of feeling that was bliss. I was no longer a bureaucrat's small, insignificant son, but one who struggled to take the measure of the world and of himself, a little champion of God and man. And all this I owed to Kafka. And for this I admired and honoured him. I realized how, because of the intensity of experience to which he had introduced me, I grew up from day to day, and became freer and better within myself. And so there was nothing finer for me than to sit beside Kafka in his office or to walk with him through the streets and gardens and alleys of Prague, and, always filled with admiration, to listen to him speaking.

In all this, I must admit, there was for me only one disturbing detail. It was the words: *Thank you, I feel very well.*

Did Kafka feel so wretched and lonely that he took flight from the intrusion of curiosity behind this stereotyped form of words? Was it a protection against the troubles of some people who visited him, and a rejection of them? Was it also directed against me?

Such thoughts always made me feel miserable and frightened. So later on I never asked Kafka how he felt and was uneasy if anyone else did in my presence and I heard Kafka lie with badly acted indifference.

On such occasions I simply could not keep still. I could not help moving nervously to and fro in the visitor's chair, playing with a button on my jacket or with my finger-nails, picking up a newspaper or a book, or – just yawning. Kafka must certainly have noticed all this and thought about it, because once – I can't remember when or what year, but the sun was shining so it must have been a bright summer's day – he suddenly explained to me the reason for the only white lie which I ever knew him to utter.

We were strolling through the Stadtpark, beyond today's central railway station, stood for a long time by the iron railings around the little lake, on whose dark waters a flock of brown-speckled and black-white-green ducks scurried about, and for a time watched the women and children around us buying rolls and laver bread from an old lame man with a massive white Father Christmas beard which stretched down to his oval sales basket, and breaking them up to throw to the ducks cackling as they swam around.

'Who, do you think, has the greater pleasure?' Kafka asked me. 'The ducks or the children?'

I replied: 'I think – the ducks. After all, they receive food, the means of survival.'

'And the children? Do they receive nothing?' Kafka looked at me reproachfully. 'Joy is food to the human soul. Without it, life is only a form of dying.'

He turned around as we walked away, and continued:

'I still remember how as a small child I wept in despair and crept into the dark corner in our dining-room between the sideboard and the linen cupboard when our nurse threatened that as a punishment for my disobedience she would not take me to the Stadtpark to see the ducks. Behind the sideboard, at that moment, I heard my heart beat with anxiety in my breast. The walk from the Kleiner Ring to the Stadtpark was in any case an immense adventure. The leading part in it was played by the gloves of our nurse who took us there. The nurse wore brown, even then slightly old-fashioned patent leather gloves. Later she bought new, crochet ones. But I didn't like them. I loved the old brown patent leather ones. So before every walk I begged her: "Please, Nanny, take your old patent leather gloves. They make it a pleasure to hold your hand." When I first said that, the girl laughed: "You're a pleasure lover!" And so indeed I was. Later I never enjoyed so deep a pleasure and joy as I did then, when the nursery maid took me by the hand to the Stadtpark to feed the ducks.'

Kafka fell silent.

We crossed by a short path to a side avenue which - lined with dense bushes and isolated trees – ran parallel to the main avenue to the edge of the grounds, so that over it one could see the upper part of the façade of what was then the Mariengasse. In this side avenue we came across what appeared to be three beggars, two men and a woman, sitting on a bench. One of them, a grey-haired, unkempt man wearing a battered bowler hat over a puce-coloured drunkard's face, was collecting the tobacco from the cigarette stumps which he was taking out of the pocket of his jacket. The tobacco which he thus obtained he stuffed into a dirty little linen sack which he held open on his lap.

Next to him sat a sun-burned old lady in a tattered green dress and a man's greasy black jacket. On her head she wore a carefully wound grey and brown print handkerchief, which covered all her hair. Her mouth – filled with strong yellow teeth – was wide open because she was in the act of conveying to her lips a cake about the shape and size of a half-brick.

Three steps away from them, his whole body bent forward, sat a shrivelled little old man with a once-green deerstalker on the back of his head and large old-fashioned wire spectacles which, as we passed him, fell down on the end of his short nose and which he three times pushed back with a mechanical gesture of his withered index finger. At the same time, he sorted out a little heap of coins which lay on his knee in a red and white check handkerchief.

As we passed, we caught a short snatch of these people's conversation, which unmistakably revealed them as beggars. The woman, her mouth still full, turned her head to the bespectacled one: 'How did things go today?'

'Not bad, not bad,' bleated the old man.

'Thank God,' gratefully added the man who was producing his tobacco supply out of cigarette stumps. 'Today was a good day. I got two bowls of soup at the Emmaus monastery.'

The woman, smiling with pleasure, leaned back. 'A nursing sister from whose hand I read a good future gave me two krone and two cakes as well.'

'What luck!' both men cried simultaneously behind our backs.

'Now, what do you think?' Kafka asked me a few steps further on. 'Are we as happy as those three on the bench?'

'I don't think so.'

'No,' said Kafka. 'We certainly haven't had such a good day.'

'I'm sure not,' I said, laughing. 'We haven't collected any tobacco in the gutters nor been given any cakes on the Karls-platz. On the other hand, we haven't foretold anyone a happy future.'

'You're joking,' Kafka complained, 'but I was being serious. Happiness does not depend on possessions. Happiness is a matter of attitude. That is to say: a happy man does not see the dark side of reality. His sense of life suppresses the gnawing woodworm of the consciousness of death. One forgets that instead of walking, one is falling. It's as if one were drugged. So it's a direct offence to be asked after one's health. It's as if one apple asked another apple: "How are the worms which the insect bites gave you?" Or as if one blade of grass asked another: "How are you withering? How goes your esteemed decomposition?" What would you think of that?'

'It would be dreadful,' I exclaimed without thinking.

'Now listen,' said Kafka, and raised his chin so high in the air that the muscles of his neck stood out like stretched ropes.

'Inquiries about one's health increase one's consciousness of dying, to which as a sick man I am particularly exposed.'

I heard the deep breath he drew through his nostrils.

'Perhaps things aren't so bad,' I said helplessly. 'You oughtn't to think about your illness.'

'That's what I tell myself and so already think of it. I cannot forget it. I have nothing which would drive it out of my mind. I lack an honest occupation.'

'How can that be?' I said, slightly irritated. 'After all, you have your position in the Insurance Institution, where you are highly regarded . . .'

But Kafka interrupted me: 'That is not an occupation, it is a form of decomposition. Every really active purposeful life, which completely fulfils a man, has the force and splendour of a flame. But what do I do? I sit in the office. It is a foul-smelling factory of pain, in which there is no sense of happiness. And so I quite calmly lie to those who inquire after my health, instead of turning away like a condemned man – which is in fact what I am.'

*

I gave Franz Kafka an account of a lecture on the situation in Russia, which had been arranged by the Union of Marxist Students in the Rosa Halls[56] of the social democratic House of the People in the Hybernergasse, and which I had attended with my father. When I finished my account, Franz Kafka said:

'I understand nothing about politics. Of course, that is a fault, which I should be glad to correct. But then I have so many faults! Even the most commonplace matters always elude me. How I admire Max Brod, who knows his way about even in the underworld of politics. He talks to me very often and at great length about the affairs of the day. I listen to him as I am listening to you, and yet – I can never get to the heart of the matter.'

'Did I not express myself clearly?'

'You misunderstand me. You expressed yourself well. The fault is mine. The war, the revolution in Russia, and the misery of the whole world seem to me like a flood of evil. It is an inundation. The war has opened the flood gates of chaos. The buttresses of human existence are collapsing. Historical development is no longer determined by the individual but by the masses. We are shoved, rushed, swept away. We are the victims of history.'

'You mean, that man no longer has a part in creating the world?'

Kafka made a few slight swaying movements with his body.

'You again misunderstand me. On the contrary, man has rejected his partnership and joint responsibility in the world.'

'That cannot be possible. Do you not see the growth of the working-class movement? The mobility of the masses?'

[My remark was an echo of the lecture on the situation in Russia and my father's comments on it.]

'That's just it,' said Franz Kafka. 'Their movement deprives us of the possibility of seeing. Our consciousness is shrinking. Without noticing it, we are losing consciousness, without losing life.'

'So you mean that men are becoming irresponsible?'

Franz Kafka smiled bitterly.

'We all live as if each of us were a dictator. And thereby we sink into beggary.'

'Where will it lead?'

Kafka shrugged his shoulders and looked out of the window.

'Our answers are only hopes and promises. But there is no certainty.'

'But without any certainty, what is life itself?'

'It is a fall. Perhaps it is the fall into sin.'

'What is sin?'

Kafka moistened his lower lip with the tip of his tongue before he answered.

'What is sin? . . . We know the word and the practice, but the sense and the knowledge of sin have been lost. Perhaps that is itself damnation, God-forsakenness, meaninglessness.'

The entry of my father interrupted our conversation.

As I was going Kafka said to me with a note of apology in his voice:

'Do not brood on what I have said to you.'

I was surprised. Kafka was to me a teacher and a father confessor. I was taken aback and said to him:

'Why? You meant it all seriously.'

He smiled.

'That is just why. My seriousness might act like poison on you. You are young.'

I was offended.

'Youth isn't a crime. In spite of it, I am still capable of thinking.'

'I see that today we really do not understand each other. But that is a good thing. Misunderstanding is a protection against my wicked pessimism, which . . . is a sin.'

*

For Christmas 1921 my father gave me a book called *The Liberation of Man, Ideas of Freedom in Past and Present*.57 When, I think in the spring of 1923, I showed this large volume to Franz Kafka, he gazed for a long time at Arnold Böcklin's picture, *War*, and V. V. Vereschagin's, *The Pyramid of Skulls*.

'No one ever gives a true picture of war,' said Kafka. 'Usually they only show its subsidiary aspects or events – like this pyramid of skulls. Yet the terrible thing about war is the dissolution of all existing certainties and conventions. The animal and physical grows rank and stifles everything spiritual. It is like a cancer. Man no longer lives for years, months, days, hours, but only for moments. And even the moment is not really lived. Man is only conscious of it. He merely exists.'

'That is because he is near to death,' I said.

'It is because of the knowledge and the fear of death.'

'Isn't that the same thing?'

'No, it is not the same. Anyone who grasps life completely has no fear of dying. The fear of death is merely the result of an unfulfilled life. It is a symptom of betrayal.'

*

We discussed one of the numerous international conferences that followed the war.

Franz Kafka said, 'The intellectual level of these great political meetings is that of ordinary coffee-house conversation. People talk loud and long, in order to say as little as possible. The really true and interesting things are the intrigues in the background, about which not a word is mentioned.'

'So in your opinion the Press is not a servant of truth.'

A painful smile pinched the corners of Kafka's mouth.

'Truth, which is one of the few really great and precious things in life, cannot be bought. Man receives it as a gift, like love or beauty. But a newspaper is a commodity, which is bought and sold.'

'So the Press only panders to man's stupidity,' I inquired anxiously.

Franz Kafka laughed, and thrust his chin forward triumphantly.

'No, no! Everything, even lies, advances the truth. Shadows do not blot out the sun.'

*

Franz Kafka was extremely cynical about the Press. He used to smile when he saw me with a bundle of newspapers.

Once he said, 'The expression "buried away in the newspapers" really sums up the situation. The papers offer us the events of the world – stone upon stone, a clod of dirt upon a clod of dirt; a heap of earth and sand. But where is its meaning? To see history as an accumulation of events is meaningless. What matters is the significance of the events. But we shall not discover that in the newspapers: we shall only discover it in faith, in the objectivization of what seems accidental.'

*

Kafka once said – I no longer remember on what occasion – that reading the newspapers was a vice of civilization: 'It's like smoking; one has to pay the printer the price of poisoning oneself.'

Kafka was a non-smoker, yet – at least so it seemed to me – he was a passionate reader of newspapers and magazines. On his desk there were always various German, Czech and also French periodicals, and he often referred to their contents in conversation. Thus I remember exactly Kafka's appraisal of Italian Fascism, a subject to which we involuntarily turned after looking at some pictures of a line of long-legged chorus girls. This was – I think – in October or November 1922. Lying open on Kafka's desk was a large theatrical magazine published in Vienna, containing an article, illustrated with a few pictures, on the latest Paris and Berlin revues.

'Are they dancers?' I stupidly inquired, with a glance at the well-disciplined chain of chorus girls. 'No, they're soldiers,' replied Kafka. 'A revue is a military parade in disguise.'

I looked without understanding at Kafka. So he developed his theme further.

'Prussian military marches and these girls' dances have the same object. Both suppress the individual. The soldier, like the girl, is no longer a free person, but an organized unit in a group, which obeys a word of command which is fundamentally alien to them. In that way they are the ideal of all commanding officers. Nothing has to be explained, nothing improvised. The word of command is enough. The soldier and the girl both parade like puppets. This endows their commander, who in himself is insignificant, with greatness. Look at him here!' Kafka took out of the middle drawer of his desk a copy of the magazine *Die Woche*, opened it and pointed to a picture of Mussolini. 'That man has the square jowl of a lion-tamer and the glass eyes, shamming seriousness and depth, of a cheap comedian. In brief: he is a genuine ringmaster to these unpolitically-political girls, who only respond in the mass. Look at them!'

He pointed to the next page, which showed a group of grinning participants in the March on Rome. 'Look at their faces! They are true as steel because they have no need to think and yet are convinced that in Rome fat livings and overflowing flesh pots are waiting for them. Mussolini's men are not revolutionaries, they are only rebels stretching out their hands for the dishes which they can't fill for themselves.'

*

I entered Kafka's office. There was nobody there. Papers lying open, two pears on a plate, a few newspapers were evidence that he was in the building. So I sat in the 'visitor's chair' near his writing-table, picked up the *Prager Tagblatt* and began to read.

After a little while Kafka came in.

'Have you been waiting long?'

'No, I have been reading.' I showed him an article in the newspaper on the League Assembly.

Kafka made a helpless gesture.

'The League! Is it in any sense a real league of nations? It seems to me that the title League of Nations is only a disguise for a new battlefield.'

'Do you mean that the League is not a peace organization?'

'The League is a machinery for localizing the battle. The war continues, only now with other weapons. Banks take the place of divisions; the fighting capacity of finance takes the place of the war potential of industry. The League is not a league of nations: it is a stock exchange for various groups of interests.'

*

I drew Franz Kafka's interest to a long article on the reparations problem. He looked away from the newspaper, pushed his under lip slightly forward, and said:

'In the end the problem is quite simple. The only really

difficult and insoluble problems are those which we cannot formulate, because they have the difficulties of life itself as their content.'

*

We discussed a newspaper article which spoke of the poor prospects of peace in Europe.

'Yet the Peace Treaty is final,' I said.

'Nothing is final,' said Franz Kafka. 'Since Abraham Lincoln nothing is finally settled unless it is justly settled.'

'When will that be?' I asked.

'Who knows? Men are not gods. History is made out of the failures and heroism of each insignificant moment. If one throws a stone into a river, it produces a succession of ripples. But most men live without being conscious of a responsibility which extends beyond themselves. And that – I think – is at the root of our misery.'

'What do you think of the case of Max Hoelz?' I asked.

The leader of the 1921 rising in Central Germany had been arrested on the Czech side of the German frontier. The Czech government refused to extradite him to Germany.

'Can you achieve good through evil? The strength which sets itself against fate is in fact a weakness. Surrender and acceptance are much stronger. But the Marquis de Sade does not understand that.'

'The Marquis de Sade!' I exclaimed.

'Yes,' Franz Kafka nodded. 'The Marquis de Sade, whose biography you lent me, is the real patron of our era.'

'That isn't really true.'

'Yes. The Marquis de Sade can obtain pleasure only through the sufferings of others, just as the luxury of the rich is paid for by the misery of the poor.'

To cover my defeat, I dived into my brief-case and showed him some reproductions of pictures by Vincent van Gogh.

Kafka was delighted by them.

'This restaurant garden with the violet night in the background is very beautiful,' he said.58 'The others are lovely too. But the restaurant garden is wonderful. Do you know his drawings?'

'No, I do not.'

'What a pity! They are in the book of *Letters from the Asylum*. Perhaps you will find the book somewhere. I should so like to be able to draw. As a matter of fact, I am always trying to. But nothing comes of it. My drawings are purely personal picture writing, whose meaning even I cannot discover after a time.'

*

I showed him the anniversary number of a Viennese weekly paper, containing pictures of the most important events of the last fifty years.59

'That is history,' I said.

Kafka pursed his mouth.

'Why? History is even more absurd than these old pictures, since for the most part it consists of official negotiations.'

*

Two days after this conversation, I called on Kafka in his office just as he was about to leave the room with a document in his hand. I wanted to leave, but he made me stay.

'I shall be back immediately,' he said, and offered me the visitor's chair. 'Look at the newspapers for a while.'

He pushed some Czech and German papers towards me.

I picked them up, read the boldly printed headlines and glanced at a law report and the brief theatrical notes, which consisted entirely of announcements. Then I turned to the back of the paper. Under the sports news was the latest instalment of a detective serial. I had read two or three sentences of it when Kafka returned.

'I see that your cops and robbers have kept you company,' he said, with a quick glance at what I was reading.

I hastily laid the paper back on the desk. 'I've only just glanced at the rubbish.'

'Do you call rubbish the literature which earns the editor

most money?' said Kafka with simulated anger. He sat himself at his desk and continued without waiting for my answer. 'That's an important commodity. Detective stories are a narcotic which distorts the proportions of life and so stands the world on its head. Detective stories are always concerned with the solution of mysteries which are hidden behind extraordinary occurrences. But in real life it's absolutely the opposite. The mystery isn't hidden in the background. On the contrary! It stares one in the face. It's what is obvious. So we do not see it. Every-day life is the greatest detective story ever written. Every second, without noticing we pass by thousands of corpses and crimes. That's the routine of our lives. But if, in spite of habit, something does succeed in surprising us, we have a marvellous sedative in the detective story, which presents every mystery of life as a legally punishable exception. It is – in Ibsen's words – a pillar of society, a starched shirt covering the heartless immorality which nevertheless claims to be bourgeois civilization.'

*

I told Kafka my dream. President Masaryk was walking on the Quay, like a perfectly ordinary citizen. I saw him clearly, his beard, the eyeglasses, arms crossed behind his back, his loose, open, winter overcoat. Franz Kafka smiled.

'Your dream suits Masaryk's personality. You could quite easily meet the head of the state so informally. Masaryk is such a strong personality that he can almost entirely dispense with the outward attributes of power. He is without dogma, and therefore he seems so human.'

I described what happened at a meeting of the National Democrats in Karolinenthal, at which the chief speaker was the Finance Minister, Dr A. Rašin.

'He is a professional gladiator,' said Kafka. 'Down with the Germans is his battlecry, and in using it he makes himself the mouthpiece of people who have far more in common with the hated Germans who are in power than with the powerless Czech masses.'

'How is that?'

'Mountain peaks see each other. Hollows and little valleys which lie in their shadow are oblivious of each other, although they usually lie on the same contour.'

*

When the British in 1922 imprisoned Mahatma Gandhi, the outstanding personality of the Indian Congress party, Kafka said: 'Now it's plain that Gandhi's movement will win. The imprisonment of Gandhi will only give his party a greater impetus. For without martyrs every movement degenerates into a pressure group of ordinary fortune-hunters. The river becomes a pool in which all thoughts of the future decay. For ideas – like everything else in the world which has a super-personal value – only live by personal sacrifices.'

*

I found on Kafka's writing-table a pamphlet, *Očista (The Purge)*[60], directed against the Foreign Minister, Beneš.

Franz Kafka said, 'They reproach Doctor Beneš with being wealthy. That is a poor criticism. Doctor Beneš is extraordinarily able. Because of his abilities and connections he would have acquired wealth under any circumstances. It wouldn't have mattered if he sold socks or waste paper. The commodity he deals in is neither here nor there. He is a great man of the commercial world. That is what matters to him – and to the others. So that this abuse is formally quite accurate, but politically absurd. They aim at the man, without hitting his acts.'

*

Shortly before the elections in 1920, the Czech social democrats in the Accident Insurance Institution distributed a small election pamphlet containing photographs and biographies of the leading social democratic candidates. After hastily scanning the little pamphlet in Kafka's office, I asked: 'Don't you find it strange that all those people have such greedy philistine faces?'

'No,' said Kafka indifferently and swept the pamphlet into the waste-paper basket. 'They're the war profiteers of the class struggle.'

*

Certain changes in organization were to be carried out in the Workmen's Accident Insurance Institution.[61] My father was working on a memorandum on the subject. At lunch he made notes on the blank margin of his newspaper, and at night he shut himself up in the dining-room.

Kafka smiled when I told him.

'Your father is a dear elderly child,' he said. 'But so is everyone who believes in reforms. They do not see that the world picture only alters in that something dies and something is born. Something falls, and something springs up. That changes the arrangement of the splinters in the kaleidoscope. But only very small children believe that they have reconstructed the toy.'

*

My father spoke about Franz Kafka with great reserve. From his remarks one might gather that my father was interested in Kafka, but always with the feeling that he did not quite understand him. Franz Kafka, on the other hand, not only respected my father but had a deep understanding of him.

'Your father always surprises me by his versatility,' he said. 'Things are so real to him. Everything is so near and intimate. He must be a man of deep faith, otherwise he could not come so near to what seem to be the simplest things in the world.'

I told him that my father devoted his spare time to carpentry and to locksmith's work. I described his enthusiasm and ambition as a craftsman with humorous exaggeration. But my manner did not appeal to Franz Kafka. He drew his eyebrows together, pushed his underlip forward, gazed at me sternly, and said:

'Don't laugh! Do not behave as if you wished to close your eyes to what is beautiful. You are only disguising your pride. For you are proud of your father. And rightly. He is so moving and creative because he has no vanity. But this fact embarrasses you. You laugh, because it hurts you that you cannot join your father in his carpentry and metalwork. Your smiles? They are unshed tears.'

*

'I have been reading Werfel's poetic drama, *Mirrorman*.'[62]

'I have known the play for a long time,' said Kafka. 'Twice Werfel has read aloud parts of it to us. The words sound well, but – to be quite candid – I do not understand the play. Werfel is a vessel with thick walls. It emits sound much more readily as a result of various forms of mechanical percussion from without than because of the ferment within.'

'Is it true that he is writing a long novel about music?' I asked.

Kafka nodded.

'Yes, he has been working on it for a long time. It is to be a novel about Verdi and Wagner. He will certainly read parts of it to us as soon as he returns to Prague.'[63]

'You say that with such a depressed expression,' I said. 'Do you not like Werfel?'

'Oh, yes, I even like him very much,' said Franz Kafka emphatically. 'I knew him even as a schoolboy. Max Brod, Felix Weltsch, Werfel, and I often went on excursions together. He was the youngest of us, and therefore perhaps the most serious. His youth boiled over within him. He read us his poems. We lay in the grass and blinked at the sun. It was such a splendid time that the mere memory of it makes me love Werfel, like my other companions of those days.'

'You sound sad,' I said.

Kafka smiled, as if he wished to apologize.

'Happy memories taste much better mixed with grief. So in fact I am not sad, but only greedy for pleasure.'

'These are the bitter roots Franz Blei speaks of.'

We both laughed, but only for a moment.

Franz Kafka immediately became serious again.

'In reality, it is not so at all,' he said. 'When I think that I understand nothing about my great friends' greatest passion, about music, a kind of gentle bitter-sweet sadness takes hold of me. It is only a breath of wind, an air of death. In a moment it has gone. Yet it makes me realize how illimitably far away I am from even those who are nearest to me, and so an evil look comes on my face, for which you must forgive me.'

'What have I to forgive? You have done me no harm. On the contrary, I should apologize for my questions.'

Kafka laughed.

'The simplest solution; the blame shall be shared with you. I shall infect you.'

Kafka opened the drawer of his desk and reached out to me a gay little volume published by the Insel Verlag.

'*Tales the Desert Fathers and Monks Told.*'[64] I read the title aloud.

'It is charming,' said Kafka. 'I enjoyed it enormously. The monks are in the desert; but the desert is not in them. It is music! There is no need to give me the book back.'

*

Franz Kafka could suddenly illuminate controversial subjects by a single remark. Yet he never tried to appear intellectual, or even witty. Whatever he said seemed, in his mouth, simple, obvious, and natural. This was not the effect of any special conjunction of words, of his play of features, or of his tone of voice. It was Kafka's whole personality which affected the listener. He was so quiet and calm. Yet his eyes were lively and brilliant, though they began to blink if, to his helpless embarrassment, I mentioned music or his own literary work in our conversations.

'Music for me is rather like the sea,' he once said. 'I am overpowered, wonderstruck, enthralled, and yet afraid, so terribly afraid of its endlessness. I am in fact a bad sailor. Max Brod is quite different. He dives head first into the flood of sound. He is a Channel swimmer.'

'Max Brod is a lover of music?'

'He understands music, as few people ever have. At least, that is what Vitězslav Novák[65] says.'

'Do you know Novák?'

Kafka nodded.

'Slightly. Novák and many other Czech composers and musicians are with Max continually. They like him very much. And he them. He helps them all, whenever he has a chance. That is what Max is like.'

'So Max Brod must speak good Czech.'

'Excellent. I envy him. Look . . .'

He opened a pigeon-hole in his desk.

'Here are two complete annual volumes of the review *Naše Reč* (*Our Language*).[66] I read it and study it ardently. What a pity that I don't possess all the previous issues. I should love to have them. Language is the music and breath of home. I – but I am badly asthmatic, since I can speak neither Czech nor Hebrew. I am learning both. But that is as if one were pursuing a dream. How can one find outside oneself something which ought to come from within?'

Kafka closed the pigeon-hole of his desk.

'The Karpfengasse in the Jewish quarter, where I was born, is immeasurably far from home.'

'I was born in Yugoslavia,' I said, because I was upset by the expression in his eyes.

But Franz Kafka slowly shook his head.

'From the Jewish quarter to the Teinkirche is much, much farther. I come from another world.'

*

Once – I don't remember the exact date – we were strolling one afternoon from the Altstädter Ring along the Pariser Strasse to the Moldau. Kafka suddenly halted opposite the Old Synagogue and said, without any relevance to the preceding conversation: 'Do you see the Synagogue? It's overlooked by all the surrounding hills. Among the modern houses surrounding it, it's only an ancient anomaly, an alien body. So is everything Jewish. That is the reason for the hostile tensions which always condense into violent outbursts of aggression. The ghetto – in my opinion – was originally a drastic act of liberation. The Jews wished to cut off their environment from the unknown, to relax the tension by erecting their ghetto walls.'

I interrupted him. 'Of course, that was foolish. The ghetto walls only strengthened what lay outside them. The walls have gone, anti-semitism remains.'

'The walls have been replaced within,' said Kafka. 'The synagogue already lies below ground level. But men will go further. They will try to grind the synagogue to dust by destroying the Jews themselves.'

'No, I don't believe it,' I exclaimed. 'Who would do such a thing?' Kafka turned his face to me. It was sad and withdrawn. There was no light in his eyes.

'The Czechs are not anti-semitic,' I said. 'They would never let themselves be led into pogroms. They are not drug addicts of extremist ideologies.'

'That is right,' said Kafka, beginning to walk again. 'But the Czechs themselves are only a little anomaly within the living space of the great powers. For that reason, there have been many attempts to undermine their spirit. First their language was meant to disappear and then the people. Yet one cannot by violence abolish what has sprung from the dust of the earth. The original seed of all being and all things always remains. The dust is eternal.'

From Kafka's compressed lips there came an indefinable sound. I don't know whether it was a short growl or a bitter laugh. I looked him inquiringly in the face. But he began to talk to me about my stamp collection.

*

On another occasion, when we happened to speak about the Czech linguistic purists, he said:

'The greatest difficulty of the Czech language is to demarcate it properly from other languages. It is young, and therefore one must protect it carefully.'

*

'Music creates new, subtler, more complicated, and therefore more dangerous pleasures,' Franz Kafka said once. 'But poetry aims at clarifying the wilderness of pleasures, at intellectualizing, purifying, and therefore humanizing them. Music is a multiplication of sensuous life; poetry, on the other hand, disciplines and elevates it.'

*

I tried to explain the intellectual content of a play which I had been reading.

'And all this is simply stated?' asked Kafka.

'No,' I answered. 'The author tries to present these ideas concretely.'

He nodded quickly.

'Quite right. Simply to say something is not enough. One must live it. And for this language is an essential intermediary, something living, a medium. Yet language also must not be used as a means but must be experienced, suffered. Language is an eternal mistress.'

*

Of an anthology of expressionist poetry[67] he said:

'The book depresses me. These poets stretch out their hands to people. But the people see, not friendly hands, but violently clenched fists aimed at their eyes and their hearts.'

*

We talked about Plato's *Laws*, which I had read in the edition published by the Eugen Diederich Verlag.

I objected to Plato's exclusion of the poet from the community of the state.

Kafka said, 'That is perfectly reasonable. Poets try to give men a different vision, in order to change reality. For that reason they are politically dangerous elements, because they want to make a change. For the state, and all its devoted servants, want only one thing, to persist.'

*

As we were walking along the Graben, in the window of Neugebauer's bookshop we saw a small black and white invitation to a lecture by the theosophist Rudolf Steiner.[68]

Kafka asked me if I knew about him.

'No,' I said. 'All I know is that he exists. My father thinks that he's a mystagogue who fabricates a pleasant substitute for religion for rich people.'

Kafka was silent. Apparently he was considering what I had said, because as we turned into the Herrengasse, he declared: 'The idea of a "substitute for religion" is a terrible one. I don't mean to say that such a thing doesn't exist. On the contrary; there's a long line of substitute religions, each one a particular form of illusion and superstition.'

'How would you distinguish the illusion from the truth?'

'By practice. A myth becomes true and effective by daily use, otherwise it only remains a bewildering play of fantasy. For that reason, every myth is bound up with the practical exercise of a rite. The practice of religion becomes simplified yet it is not something simple. It demands sacrifice. First of all, one has to surrender something of one's comfort. That doesn't suit people for whom, as they say, life is easy. So they look for a comfortable substitute. Your father is right. But can there be any substitute for fundamental truth?'

'No!' I concurred. 'It's a mystification.'

'Of course. Like air to the body, truth is indispensable to the soul and so to the body also.' He smiled. 'In the creation, there's no division of labour. There it's a matter of the one and the many at the same time. The division into special spheres is an invention of men who fear the ocean of the All, of yesterday, today and tomorrow. Theosophy, the love of a meaning, is in fact nothing but the love of the whole. Men search for a way.'

'Does Steiner reveal it?' I asked. 'Is he a prophet or a charlatan?'

'I don't know,' declared Kafka. 'I'm not clear in my mind about him. He is an uncommonly eloquent man. But this is a talent which also belongs to the armoury of the trickster. I'm not saying that Steiner is a trickster. But he could be. Deceivers always try to solve difficult problems on the cheap. The problem with which Steiner is concerned is the most difficult one there is. It is the dark division between consciousness and being, the tension between the circumscribed drop of water and the infinite sea. I believe that in this matter Goethe's view is the right one. One must, with quiet respect for the unknowable, accept the order of everything that is knowable. The smallest thing, like the greatest, must be close and precious to one.'

'Is that also Steiner's view?'

Kafka shrugged his shoulders and said: 'I don't know. But perhaps that's my fault, not his. Steiner is alien to me. I cannot get close to him. I am too involved in myself.'

'You're a chrysalis!' I said, laughing.

'Yes,' Kafka said seriously, 'I'm caught in an iron-hard web, without the slightest hope that one day a butterfly may fly out of my cocoon. But that also is only my own fault – or to put it better – it's the ever-recurrent sin of despair.'

'And your writings?'

'They're only attempts, scraps of paper thrown to the winds.'

We had reached the corner opposite the general post office.

Kafka extended his hand. – 'Forgive me. I have an appointment with Brod—' and with long strides hurried across the road.

*

I accompanied Franz Kafka home from his office.

At the entrance to his parents' house we unexpectedly met Felix Weltsch, Max Brod and his wife. They exchanged a few words and arranged to meet in the evening at Oskar Baum's.

When Kafka's friends had left us, he remembered suddenly that I had never met Brod's wife before.

'And I didn't introduce you properly,' he said. 'I am really very sorry.'

'It doesn't matter,' I said. 'I could at least look at her all the better.'

'Did you like her?'

'She has wonderful blue eyes,' I said.

Kafka was astonished.

'You noticed that at once?'

'I make a study of eyes. They tell me more than words,' I said pompously.

But Franz Kafka did not hear. He gazed gravely into the distance.

'All my friends have wonderful eyes,' he said. 'The light of their eyes is the only illumination of the dark dungeon in which I live. And even that is only artificial light.'

He laughed, gave me his hand, and went into the house.

*

He once said about insomnia, from which he suffered:

'Perhaps my insomnia only conceals a great fear of death. Perhaps I am afraid that the soul – which in sleep leaves me – will never return. Perhaps insomnia is only an all too vivid sense of sin, which is afraid of the possibility of a sudden judgement. Perhaps insomnia is itself a sin. Perhaps it is a rejection of the natural.'

I remarked that insomnia is an illness.

Kafka replied, 'Sin is the root of all illness. That is the reason for mortality.'

*

I went with Kafka to an exhibition of French painting in the gallery on the Graben.

There were some pictures by Picasso: cubist still-lifes and rose-coloured women with gigantic feet.

'He is a wilful distortionist,' I said.

'I do not think so,' said Kafka. 'He only registers the deformities which have not yet penetrated our consciousness. Art is a mirror, which goes "fast", like a watch – sometimes.'

*

In the spring of 1921, two automatic photographic machines, recently invented abroad, were installed in Prague, which reproduced six or ten or more exposures of the same person on a single print.

When I took such a series of photographs to Kafka I said light-heartedly: 'For a couple of krone one can have oneself photographed from every angle. The apparatus is a mechanical *Know-Thyself*.'

'You mean to say, the *Mistake-Thyself*,' said Kafka, with a faint smile.

I protested: 'What do you mean? The camera cannot lie!'

'Who told you that?' Kafka leaned his head towards his shoulder. 'Photography concentrates one's eye on the superficial. For that reason it obscures the hidden life which glimmers through the outlines of things like a play of light and shade. One can't catch that even with the sharpest lens. One has to grope for it by feeling. Or do you think that one can successfully apprehend the profound depths of this ever-returning reality, before which, through all former ages, whole legions of poets, artists, scientists and other miracle workers have stood in trembling longing and hope, by pressing the knob of a cheap machine? – I doubt it. This automatic camera doesn't multiply men's eyes but only gives a fantastically simplified fly's eye view.'

*

I took him photographs of constructivist pictures.

Kafka said, 'They are merely dreams of a marvellous America, of a wonderland of unlimited possibilities. That is perfectly understandable, because Europe is becoming more and more a land of impossible limitations.'

*

We saw a collection of political drawings by George Grosz.[69]

'What hatred!' I said.

Franz Kafka gave a strange smile.

'Disappointed youth,' he said. 'It is a hatred which springs from the impossibility of love. The force of expression comes from a perfectly definite weakness. That is the source of the despair and violence in these drawings. What is more, in some annual I have seen poems by Grosz.'

Kafka pointed to the drawings.

'They are literature in pictures.'

*

Franz Kafka sometimes insisted, with a vehemence which reminded one of the passionate obstinacy of fanatical Talmudists, on the narrow literal meaning of ideas, which for him were not sound-symbols for things, but were themselves independent and indestructible truths.

'Words must be exactly and strictly defined,' he said to me once, 'otherwise we may fall into entirely unexpected pitfalls. Instead of ascending by clear-cut steps we may fall into shifting sand and slime.'

Thus nothing annoyed Kafka more than loose, vague and thoughtlessly babbled phrases. In such cases his voice could become extremely sharp and severe, which was something very unusual for him. The stimulus was often provided by some perfectly ordinary and unimportant word or by some incident which to anyone else would have seemed trivial.

Thus I once entered his office just as he was staring in disgust at a large brown volume which was lying on his desk. He only replied to my greeting with a curt nod of the head and then immediately said accusingly: 'Look at what they have put on my desk!'

I looked at the desk and said: 'A book.'

But he became impatient: 'Yes, a book! But in fact only a hollow, empty sham. It's made of artificial leather. That is to say, it has no trace either of art or of leather. It's only paper. And inside – look for yourself!'

He opened the book.

I saw pages of greenish-grey office paper.

'There's nothing inside it, nothing,' said Kafka excitedly. 'What is it intended for? What's the meaning of this book which isn't a book? I was only in the next-door office for a moment? When I came back this thing was already on my desk.'

'Perhaps,' I said cautiously, 'it wasn't meant for you at all. I know that Seidel, the cleaner who works in the registry, is interested in book-binding. Telephone him; perhaps he made the book up for someone.'

Kafka took my advice, seized the telephone and learned that Seidel had put the artificial leather book on the desk for Treml, because Kafka's colleague from time to time ordered such books with blank pages for his private use.

That appeased Kafka. He placed his hands with outstretched fingers on the desk and looked in amazement at the artificial leather book, which I placed on Treml's table. Then he slowly turned his face to me, laughed like a small, shy schoolboy, and said in a soft voice, subdued by an inner conflict: 'My behaviour looked rather absurd to you. But I can't help myself. All false appearances frighten me. The As-If is always a mark of evil. It leaps to the eye. There is nothing worse than pretence, which converts every effect into its opposite.'

*

I don't know how the cinema business was regulated in pre-war Austria-Hungary. But in the first Czechoslovak Republic, one could only operate a cinema if one had a special cinema concession. However, in principle permission was not granted to individual persons but only to 'national legal entities', such as, for instance, fire brigades, athletic clubs and 'other organs of the community', which usually subcontracted to commercial firms in return for a fee or a share in the profits.

A cinema concession, therefore, had an exchange value, whose price and yield rose year by year during the first Czechoslovak Republic, because after the sufferings of the First World War, the desire for amusement of the broad masses of the people, and therewith the number of cinemas, was profoundly stimulated. As a result, of course, the holders of cinema licences obtained from lessees large sums of money, which so tickled the vanity of the organizations concerned that they insisted on immortalizing the titles of their communal or national associations in the names of the cinemas for which they held the concessions.

So it came about that all the cinemas licensed to the Czech gymnastic association, *Sokol* (German: Falka – Falcon) were called *Sokols* in every town and village of the Republic. The Union of Czech Legionaries, which held the concession for the cinema near the Workers' Accident Insurance Institution, called it *Siberien* (Czech: Sibír) in memory of the Legion's origin in Russia. The Social Democratic party executive's cinema was called the *Lido-Bio*, an abbreviation of *Lidový Biograf* (People's Cinema).

But in addition to such easily understood names, some cinemas in the first Czechoslovak Republic had names which were quite extraordinary. Thus, for instance, the largest cinema in one important industrial centre was called the *Sanitas*, because the concession belonged to the Red Cross. Many people did not know this. On the other hand, *Sanitas* was known throughout the republic as the trade mark of a factory which manufactured trusses. The Red Cross's cinema was therefore commonly known to the wags as the *First-Aid* or the *Bandages*.

The most absurd name, however, there can ever have been for a cinema was displayed on the sign above the entrance of a small cinema in Ziskov, a working-class quarter of Prague. It proclaimed, *Cinema of the Blind* (Czech: Bio Slepcu), because the concession belonged to the association for the support of the blind.

Kafka, when I told him about the cinema, first opened his eyes wide, then the next moment laughed louder than I ever heard him do before or since.

Then he said: '*Bio Slepcu!* Every cinema should be called that. Their flickering images blind people to reality. How did you discover this blind man's cinema?'

'I work there,' I said, and told him how this had come about.

The *Cinema of the Blind* in Ziskov occupied what had formerly been an old warehouse, which had been bought and converted into a somewhat primitive cinema by a Czech emigrant who had returned from the United States. Accordingly, the natives of the district referred to it with unconcealed contempt as *The Shed*. It was not some sumptuously appointed substitute for a theatre, but merely a bare, somewhat shabby cultural food-bin, often attended by the people of the immediate neighbourhood in carpet slippers and without collars, and frequently commentating on the film as it unrolled in very coarse language.

The owner of the cinema, who at every performance stood near the orchestra (with an enormous bowler on his head), as a rule regarded these comments as a personal insult, against which he protested in a menacing voice. If then further remarks were hurled at him out of the darkness, he descended, accompanied by two stalwart chuckers-out, into the blackness of the auditorium, seized one of the commentators and thrust him to the door, usually shouting: 'Out you get! This isn't a brothel, it's a theatre. Your interruptions are an insult to all these cultured people sitting quietly in their seats. So out you go. Am I right?'

The question was directed to the audience, who immediately went into action like a Greek chorus in response to this appeal.

'Right! Chuck him out! Sock him one! Quiet! Get on with the film!'

The bold commentator was ejected to a musical accompaniment, for the little cinema orchestra calmly continued to play throughout the entire uproar. Every member of it was expressly required to when appointed. To continue to play during the battle of words and the removal of interrupters was part of their agreed contract of service, which in any case was not very favourable to them.

On weekdays there was only one evening performance at the *Cinema of the Blind*. Thus the musicians could not make a decent income, as they were only paid for the very few performances that were given. So no professional musician would play at the *Cinema of the Blind*, but only people from other occupations who simply made music as an agreeable side-line. Among them was my former schoolfellow Olda S., who by day served at the sales counter of a small chemist's shop in the

Wenzelsplatz and in the evening, as second violin in the cinema in the Ziskov warehouse, fiddled away at marches, melodies from operettas, intermezzos, operatic pot-pourris and other musical works. So when once – I cannot remember exactly when – in the *Blind Man's Cinema* the harmonium player – an elderly ex-teacher addicted to alcohol – suffered a stroke at a rehearsal and fell from his stool, so that the little orchestra found itself deprived of the substitute for a woodwind provided by the harmonium, Olda fetched me to help them out. As I possessed the requisite musical skill, I was immediately offered a contract and so for some time I operated the asthmatic, wheezing substitute woodwind which they called a harmonium.

The 20 krone which I received for each performance were to me immense wealth, and so I spent my first week's wages on having Kafka's three stories – *The Metamorphosis, The Judgement* and *The Stoker* – bound in a dark brown leather volume, with the name *Franz Kafka* elegantly tooled in gold lettering.

The book lay in the brief-case on my knee as I told Kafka about the warehouse-cinema. Then I proudly took the volume out of the case and gave it across the desk to Kafka.

'What is this?' he asked in astonishment.

'It's my first week's wages.'

'Isn't that a waste?'

Kafka's eyelids fluttered. His lips were sharply drawn in. For a few seconds he contemplated the name in the gold lettering, hastily thumbed through the pages of the book and – with obvious embarrassment – placed it before me on the desk. I was about to ask why the book offended him, when he began to cough. He took a handkerchief from his pocket, held it to his mouth, replaced it when the attack was over, stood up and went to the small washstand behind his desk and washed his hands, then said as he dried them: 'You overrate me. Your trust oppresses me.'

He sat himself at his desk and said, with his hands to his temples: 'I am no burning bush. I am not a flame.'

I interrupted him. 'You shouldn't say that. It's not just. To me, for example, you are fire, warmth and light.'

'No, no!' he contradicted me, shaking his head. 'You are wrong. My scribbling does not deserve a leather binding. It's only my own personal spectre of horror. It oughtn't to be printed at all. It should be burned and destroyed. It is without meaning.'

I became furious. 'Who told you that?' I was forced to contradict him – 'How can you say such a thing? Can you see into the future? What you are saying to me is entirely your subjective feeling. Perhaps your scribbling, as you call it, will tomorrow represent a significant voice in the world. Who can tell today?'

I drew a deep breath.

Kafka stared at the desk. At the corners of his mouth were two short, sharp lines of shadow.

I was ashamed of my outburst, so I said quietly, in a low, explanatory tone: 'Do you remember what you said to me about the Picasso exhibition?'

Kafka looked at me without understanding.

I continued: 'You said that art is a mirror which – like a clock running fast – foretells the future. Perhaps your writing is, in today's *Cinema of the Blind*, only a mirror of tomorrow.'

'Please, don't go on,' said Kafka fretfully, and covered his eyes with both hands.

I apologized. 'Please forgive me, I didn't mean to upset you. I'm stupid.'

'No, no – you're not that!' Without removing his hands, he rocked his whole body to and fro. 'You are right. You are certainly right. Probably that's why I can't finish anything. I am afraid of the truth. But can one do otherwise?' He took his hands away from his eyes, placed his clenched fists on the table and said in a low, suppressed voice: 'One must be silent, if one can't give any help. No one, through his own lack of hope, should make the condition of the patient worse. For that reason, all my scribbling is to be destroyed. I am no light. I have merely lost my way among my own thorns. I'm a dead end.'

Kafka leaned backwards. His hands slipped lifelessly from the table. He closed his eyes.

'I don't believe it,' I said with utter conviction, yet added appeasingly: 'And even if it were true, it would be worthwhile to display the dead end to people.'

Kafka merely shook his head slowly. 'No, no . . . I am weak and tired.'

'You should give up your work here,' I said gently, to relax the tension which I felt between us.

Kafka nodded. 'Yes, I should. I wanted to creep away behind this office desk, but it only increased my weakness. It's become—,' Kafka looked at me with an indescribably painful smile, '—a cinema of the blind.'

Then he closed his eyes again.

I was glad at this moment there was a knock on the door behind me.

*

I showed Kafka some new books published by the firm of Neugebauer. As he was turning the leaves of a volume with illustrations by George Grosz, he said:

'That is the familiar view of Capital – the fat man in a top hat squatting on the money of the poor.'

'It is only an allegory,' I said.

Franz Kafka drew his eyebrows together.

'You say "only"! In men's thoughts the allegory becomes an image of reality, which is naturally a mistake. But the error already exists here.'

'You mean that the picture is false?'

'I would not quite say that. It is both true and false. It is true only in one sense. It is false, in that it proclaims this incomplete view to be the whole truth. The fat man in the top hat sits on the necks of the poor. That is correct. But the fat man is Capitalism, and that is not quite correct. The fat man oppresses the poor man within the conditions of a given system. But he is not the system itself. He is not even its master. On the contrary, the fat man also is in chains, which the picture does not show. The picture is not complete. For that reason it is not good. Capitalism is a system of relationships, which go from inside to out, from outside to in, from above to below, and from below to above. Everything is relative, everything is in chains. Capitalism is a condition both of the world and of the soul.'

'Then how would you picture it?'

Kafka shrugged his shoulders and smiled sadly.

'I don't know. In any case we Jews are not painters. We cannot depict things statically. We see them always in transition, in movement, as change. We are story-tellers.'

The entry of one of the staff broke off our conversation.

When the disturbing visitor had gone, I wanted to return to the interesting topic of conversation which we had begun. Kafka, however, cut me off and said:

'Let us forget about it. A story-teller cannot talk about story-telling. He tells stories or is silent. That is all. His world begins to vibrate within him, or it sinks into silence. My world is dying away. I am burnt out.'

*

I showed him my portrait, drawn by my friend Vladimír Sychra.

Kafka was delighted with the portrait.[70]

'The drawing is wonderful. It is full of truth,' he said several times.

'Do you mean that it is true to life as a photograph is?'

'What are you thinking of? Nothing can be so deceiving as a photograph. Truth, after all, is an affair of the heart. One can get at it only through art.'

*

'The actual reality is always unrealistic,' said Franz Kafka. 'Look at the clarity, purity, and veracity of a Chinese coloured woodcut. To speak like that – that would be something!'

*

Kafka not only admired the art of ancient Chinese pictures and woodcuts; he was also charmed by the proverbs, similes and sharply pointed parables of ancient Chinese philosophy – and of the religious books which he read in the translations by the German sinologist, Richard Wilhelm-Tsingtau. This was apparent, when I once arrived at the Accident Insurance Institution with the first Czech translation of Laotse's *Tao-Te-King*. For a moment Kafka looked with interest through the pages of the little volume, printed on poor paper, then laid it on his desk and said: 'I've studied Taoism fairly deeply over a long period, so far as that's possible in translation. I possess nearly all the volumes of the German translations of this school of thought which have been published by Diedrichs in Jena.'[71]

To show me, he opened a side-drawer of his desk, from which he took five yellow volumes bound in linen and elaborately decorated with black ornamentation, which he placed on the edge of his desk. I took up each book after the other: KUNG-FUTSE, *Conversations*; TSCHUNG YUNG, *The Great Doctrine of Measure and Mean*; LAOTSE, *The Book of the Ancients regarding Sense and Life*; LIÄ TSE, *The True Book of the Spring of the First Cause*; CHUANG TSI, *The True Book of the South Land of Blossom*.

'That's a mighty treasury,' I said, as I placed the books back on top of the desk.

'Yes,' said Kafka, 'the Germans are thorough. They make a museum out of everything. These five volumes are only half the complete set.'

'Will you get the others?'

'No. What I have is enough for me. They are a sea in which one can easily drown. In Kung-Futse's conversations one is still on firm ground; but later everything dissolves more and more into darkness, Laotse's sayings are nuts that are hard as stones to crack. I am fascinated by them, but their kernel remains hidden from me. I've re-read them several times. I discovered that – like a little boy playing with glass marbles – I followed them from one cranny of thought to another without in any way getting any further. In these aphoristic marbles, I only discovered the hopeless shallowness of my own intellectual categories, which couldn't define or accommodate Laotse's marbles. That was a rather depressing discovery, so I gave up playing marbles. Actually, I've only half understood and half digested only one of these books. That's the one about the southern land of blossom.'

Kafka took up the book inscribed Chuang Tsi, turned its pages for a few moments, and then said, 'I've underlined some sentences. For instance: *Death is not brought to life by life*; *Life is not killed by dying. Life and death are conditioned*; *they are contained within a great coherence*. This is, I think, the fundamental and central problem of all religions and of wisdom about life. It's a question of grasping the coherence of things and time, of deciphering oneself, and of penetrating one's own becoming and dying. Here, a few sentences later, I've underlined an entire passage.' He held the book out to me; on page 167 the following passage was framed by four thick pencil strokes:

The men of antiquity changed outwardly, but inwardly remained unchanged. Today men change inwardly but outwardly remain unchanged. When men change by adapting themselves to circumstance yet remain one and the same, that is not really change. One remains calm in changing and calm in not changing; men remain calm in all their contacts with the outside world and do not let themselves be drawn into the multiplicity of things. Thus men believed in the gardens and halls of the wise men of old. But the gentlemen who gathered together in the different schools of learning fought against each other with assertion and counter-assertion. And today, for the first time, how do things look? The saint who is called dallies in the world but does not injure the world.

I returned the book to Kafka, and looked at him inquiringly, in expectation of some explanatory commentary. But since he closed the book without a word, and returned it to the drawer with the other yellow volumes, I said slightly plaintively: 'I don't understand that. Quite honestly, the passage is too deep for me.'

Kafka stiffened. He looked at me quietly with his head on one side for a few moments, then said slowly. 'That's quite normal. The truth is always an abyss. One must – as in a swimming pool – dare to dive from the quivering springboard of trivial everyday experience and sink into the depths, in order later to rise again – laughing and fighting for breath – to the now doubly illuminated surface of things.'

Kafka laughed like a happy summer excursionist. He would certainly have explained to me the pencil-framed passage in the book. But we were disturbed. My father came for me, in order to send me on various errands. So I was left to hope that perhaps some time later Kafka would return to the subject of the ancient Chinese philosophers.

To strengthen my faith in such a possibility, I bought Chuang Tsi's book, which was extremely expensive for me in my existing circumstances, marked in pencil the passage under-lined by Kafka, and then carried the book continually around with me in my brief-case, so that I might have it immediately at hand in the event of a further discussion. But it never arose. Kafka never again mentioned *The True Book of the South Land of Blossom*. So I placed the translation, which I had bought at such a sacrifice, in my bookshelf, where it was quickly over-shadowed by the charm of new literary discoveries. Kafka, however, despite his silence, seemed to be still occupied with the subject of Taoism. This is proved by two little books which are still in my possession today: *Man, become Essence! Sayings of Laotse*, translated into German by Klabund; and *Laotse's Tao-te-King* in F. Fiedler's translation. I was given them by Kafka, who shrugged his shoulders in embarrassment when I asked him about Gustav Wyneken, the publisher of Fiedler's translation.

Then he said: 'He is the founder and high priest of the German *Wandervogel*. Gustav Wyneken and his friends wish to escape from the grip of our machine world. They turn to nature and to man's most ancient intellectual heritage. They spell out – as you can see here – transcriptions of reality from translations of ancient Chinese instead of quietly reading the original text of their own lives and responsibilities. To them the day before yesterday seems more accessible than today. But reality is never and nowhere more accessible than in the immediate moment of one's own life. It's only there that it can be won or lost. All it guarantees us is what is superficial, the façade. But one must break through this. Then everything becomes clear.'

Kafka smiled, but I asked, with furrowed brow:

'But how does one do that? How does one proceed? Is there some sure guide?'

'No, there is none,' said Kafka, shaking his head. 'There is no route map of the way to truth. The only thing that counts is to make the venture of total dedication. A prescription would already imply a withdrawal, mistrust, and therewith the beginning of a false path. One must accept everything patiently and fearlessly. Man is condemned to life, not to death.'

His face was suffused by an enchanting, boyish smile as he added the following lightly spoken phrases in Czech and German to his hitherto gravely enunciated sentences: 'Kdo se bojí, nesmí do lesa. Ale v lese jame vsichni. Kazdý jinde e jinak. (One who is afraid should not go into the wood. But we are all in the wood. Everyone in a different way and in a different place.) There's only one thing certain. That is one's own inadequacy. One must start from that.'

*

Once when I was talking to my father about Kafka, he described him as a thoroughgoing Do-it-yourself man. He said: 'Kafka would like to knead his own daily bread and bake it in his own oven. He'd also like to make his own clothes. He cannot bear anything artificial. Stock phrases arouse his suspicion. For him convention is merely a mental and verbal uniform, which he rejects as a degrading form of prison dress. Kafka is an individualist through and through, a man who cannot share the burden of existence with anyone else. He walks by himself. He is deliberately and by his own choice a solitary. In this respect, he is openly militant.'

A few days later, a small incident occurred in Kafka's office which confirmed my father's words.

A long column of spick and span soldiers, with flags waving and blaring brass band, was marching past the Accident

Insurance Institution. Kafka, my father and I were standing at the open window. My father photographed the march past. He mounted his camera in the most varied positions and was greatly concerned about the result of his photographic exertions. Kafka watched him with a gentle, indefinable smile.

My father noticed this and said: 'I have now used up six double reels of film. Among the twelve shots perhaps – I believe – there might be something decent.'

'A pity about the subject,' said Kafka. 'The whole affair is so boring.'

'What do you mean?' said my father in astonishment.

'It's certainly nothing new,' answered Kafka and went to his desk. 'As a matter of fact armies only have one slogan: *Forward on behalf of all those who sit behind us at the cash desks and writing tables!* For modern armies, the true ideals of humanity do not lie ahead, as an objective, but in the rear, where everything human has been betrayed.'

My father gazed at the ground in perplexity. He only found his tongue again when Kafka had seated himself at his desk. Then he said: 'You are a rebel.'

'Unfortunately,' said Kafka, 'I am engaged in the most destructive and almost completely hopeless rebellion there could ever be.'

'Against whom?' asked my father.

'Against myself,' answered Kafka with half-shut eyes, and leaned back in his chair. 'Against my own limitations and apathy. In the end, therefore, against this desk and the chair I'm sitting in.'

Kafka gave a tired smile.

His expression was reflected in my father's, who tried to save himself by smiling with him, but did not succeed very well; his lips fell into two anxious folds, his eyelids trembled. Kafka, who must have noticed this, handed my father some office papers. He tried to counter my father's low spirits with a few factual remarks about the papers. He was even successful. My father left the office with me laughing dutifully. Then after a few steps he suddenly said in the corridor: That's him all over!

'What is?' I asked.

'His nature! That's what he's like,' muttered my father. 'With a few words he can make people look fools in their own eyes. One feels like – like a jack-in-the-box stuffed with empty phrases. One can't blame him for it. All that photographing of mine was a piece of nonsense. I'd rather expose all the shots I have in this box and wipe them all out.'

*

We looked at Josef Čapek's linocuts in the left-wing periodical *Cerven* (*June*).[72]

'I cannot quite understand the form of expression,' I said.

'Then you do not understand the content either,' said Franz Kafka. 'The form is not the expression of the content but only its power of attraction, the door and the way to the content. If it succeeds, then the hidden background also reveals itself.'

*

When, after the First World War, the first great American films, among them Charlie Chaplin's short comedies, appeared in Prague, Ludwig Venclík, then a young film fan and today a film director, gave me a large bundle of American film magazines together with a few publicity stills from Chaplin's films.

Kafka, to whom I showed the pictures, looked at them with an affectionate smile.

'You're familiar with Chaplin?' I asked.

'Only slightly,' Kafka answered. 'I've seen one or two of his grotesques.'

He looked long and seriously at the stills, which I had placed before him, and then said reflectively: 'That's a very energetic, work-obsessed man. There burns in his eyes the flame of despair at the unchangeable condition of the oppressed, yet he does not capitulate to it. Like every genuine comedian, he has the bite of a beast of prey, and he uses it to attack the world. He does it in his own unique way. Despite the white face and the black eyebrows, he's not a sentimental Pierrot, nor is he some snarling critic. Chaplin is a technician. He's the man of a machine world, in which most of his fellow men no longer command the requisite emotional and mental equipment to make the life allotted to them really their own. They do not have the imagination. As a dental technician makes false teeth, so he manufactures aids to the imagination. That's what his films are. That's what films in general are.'

'My friend, who gave me the stills, tells me that a whole series of Chaplin films is to be shown at the film centre. Would you like to go with me? Venclík would certainly be glad to take us.'

'Thank you, no. I would rather not,' said Kafka, shaking his head. 'Jokes are far too serious a matter for me. I could quite easily stand there like a completely painted clown.'

*

Franz Kafka gave me some issues of a review, *The Brenner*, which contained essays by Theodore Haecker, translations of Kierkegaard, and also Carl Dallago's essays on Giovanni Segantini.[73]

Reading it aroused my interest in this painter of the Southern Alps. So I was very pleased when my friend, the young actor Franz Lederer, gave me Segantini's *Writings and Letters*. I showed the book to Kafka, and drew his attention especially to the following paragraph, which pleased me greatly:

'Art is not that truth which is and exists outside of us. That has, and can have, no value as art; it is, and can only be, a blind imitation of nature, that is to say, simply giving back to nature her own material. But the material must be worked on by the spirit before it can develop into eternal art.'

Franz Kafka gave me the book back across his writing-table, for a moment looked into space, then turned to me impetuously:

'The material must be worked on by the spirit? What does that mean? It means to experience, nothing else except to experience and to master what is experienced. That is what matters.'

*

Franz Kafka always gave a look of surprise when I told him I had been to the cinema. Once I reacted to this change of expression by asking:

'Don't you like the cinema?'

After a moment's thought Kafka replied:

'As a matter of fact I've never thought about it. Of course it is a marvellous toy. But I cannot bear it, because perhaps I am too "optical" by nature. I am an Eye-man. But the cinema disturbs one's vision. The speed of the movements and the rapid change of images force men to look continually from one to another. Sight does not master the pictures, it is the pictures which master one's sight. They flood one's consciousness. The cinema involves putting the eye into uniform, when before it was naked.'

'That is a terrible statement,' I said. 'The eye is the window of the soul, a Czech proberb says.'

Kafka nodded.

'Films are iron shutters.'

A few days later I returned to this conversation.

'The cinema is a terrible power,' I said. 'It is far more powerful than the Press. Shopgirls, models, seamstresses, all have faces like Barbara La Marr, Mary Pickford, and Pearl White.'

'That is quite natural. The desire for beauty turns women into actresses. Real life is only a reflection of the dreams of poets. The strings of the lyre of modern poets are endless strips of celluloid.'

*

We talked about a literary inquiry carried out by a Prague newspaper, which began with the question: Is there a young Art?

I said, 'Isn't it odd, to search for a young art? There is only art or trash, which often hides under the masks of various -isms and fashions.'

Franz Kafka said, 'The point of the question is not in the substantive "Art", but in the limiting term "young". From this it is clear that there are serious doubts about the very existence of an artistic younger generation. And indeed today it is difficult

to conceive of a younger generation which is free and un-
burdened. The terrible flood of these last years has drowned
everything. Even the children. Of course, corruption and youth
mutually exclude each other. But what is the youth of men
of today? It is the friend and intimate of corruption. Men
know the power of corruption. But they have forgotten the
power of youth. Therefore they are in doubt about youth itself.
And can there be art without the ecstasy of the confidence of
youth?'

Franz Kafka stretched out his arms, then let them drop as if
paralysed into his lap.

'Youth is weak. The pressure from without is so strong. To
defend and at the same time dedicate onself – it causes a
convulsion that shows on one's face like a grimace. The
language of young artists today hides more than it reveals.'

I told him that the young artists whom I had met at Lydia
Holzner's were usually people of about forty.

Franz Kafka nodded.

'That would be so. Many men are now recovering their youth
for the first time. For the first time they are passing through the
cowboy-and-Indian stage. Naturally, not so that they scamper
along the paths of the municipal park armed with bows and
arrows. No! They sit in the cinema and watch adventure films.
That's all it is. The darkened cinema is the magic lantern of
their wasted youth.'

*

In conversation about young writers Franz Kafka said:

'I envy the young.'

I said, 'You are not so old yourself.'

Kafka smiled.

'I am as old as Jewry, as the wandering Jew.'

I gave him a look out of the corner of my eye.

Kafka put his arm round my shoulder.

'Now you are shocked. That was only a miserable effort to
make a joke. But I really do envy youth. The older one grows,
the larger one's horizon. But the possibilities of life grow

smaller and smaller. In the end, one can give only one look upwards, give one breath outwards. At that moment a man probably surveys his whole life. For the first time – and the last time.'

*

I brought Kafka a special edition of the Prague Czech magazine *Cerven* (June), containing a translation of the rhythmically flowing poem *La Zone* by Guillaume Apollinaire. But Kafka knew the poem already.

He said: 'I read the translation soon after it appeared. I also knew the French original. It appeared in the book of poems, *Alcools*. Those poems, and a cheap new edition of Flaubert's letters, were the first French books I held in my hand after the war.'[74]

I asked: 'What impression did they make on you?'

'Which? Apollinaire's poem or Čapek's translation?' - Kafka clarified my question in his own sharp, decisive way.

'Both!' I declared, and immediately gave my own opinion. 'I'm overcome by them.'

'I can quite imagine it,' said Kafka. 'They're a verbal masterpiece. Both the poem and the translation.'

That set me going. I was pleased that my 'discovery' had Kafka's approval and so I tried to propagate and explain my enthusiasm. I quoted the lines from the beginning of the poem in which Apollinaire addresses the Eiffel Tower as the shepherdess of a flock of traffic-jammed motor-cars, mentioned the clock with the Hebrew numbers on the Jewish town hall in Prague to which he refers, recited his description of the agate and malachite walls of St Vitus's Cathedral on the Hradschin, and brought my judgement on Apollinaire's work to a climax with the words: 'The poem is a great bridge cantilevered from the Eiffel Tower to the St Vitus Cathedral and spans the whole multicoloured phenomenal world of our time.'

'Yes,' said Kafka, 'the poem is really a work of art. Apollinaire has combined his visual experiences into a kind of revelation. He is a virtuoso.'

The last sentence was filled with a peculiar, ambivale
I felt that there was beneath the words of admiration an unspoken, yet clearly apparent reservation, which, against my
will, found a gently swelling echo in myself.

'A virtuoso?' I said slowly. 'I don't like the sound of that.'

'Nor do I.' Kafka took me up directly and – as it seemed to
me – with relief. 'I am against all virtuosity. The virtuoso rises
above his subject because of his juggler's facility. But can a poet
be superior to his subject? No! He is held captive by the world
he has experienced and portrayed, as God is by his own
creation. To liberate himself from it, he places it outside himself. That's not an act of virtuosity. It's a birth, an addition to
life, like all births. Have you ever heard it said of a woman that
she is a virtuoso in child-bearing?'

'No, I haven't. The words Birth and Virtuosity don't suit
each other.'

'Of course not,' Kafka agreed. 'There are no virtuoso births.
There are only difficult or easy, but in every case painful, ones.
Virtuosity is the monopoly of comedians. But they always
start where the artist leaves off. One can see that in Apollinaire's
poem. He concentrates his different experiences in space into a
super-personal vision of time. What Apollinaire displays for us
is a film in words. He is a juggler, who conjures up for the
reader an entertaining picture. No poet does that, only a
comedian, a juggler. The poet tries to ground his vision in the
daily experience of the reader. You can see that, for instance,
in this.'

Kafka reached into a side drawer of his desk and placed
before me a small grey-green pasteboard-covered book. 'These
are Kleist's stories,' he said. 'They are genuine poetry. In them,
the language is perfectly clear. You'll find no verbal flourishes,
nothing pretentious. Kleist is not a juggler or an emotion-
monger. His whole life was spent under the pressure of the
visionary tension between man and fate, which he illuminated
and held fast in clear universally intelligible language. His
vision was meant to become a universal existential value
accessible to everybody. He aimed to achieve this without

verbal aerobatics, commentaries and illusions. In Kleist, modesty, understanding and patience combined to create a strength which is necessary for any successful birth. For that reason I read him again and again. Art is not a matter of a sleight-of-hand which disappears in a flash, but of an example which has an effect over a long period. You can see that quite clearly in Kleist's stories. They are the root of the whole of modern Germany's art of language.'

*

Richard Hülsenbeck, the leader of Dadaism in Germany, gave a lecture in Prague.

I wrote a report on it and gave the manuscript to Kafka.

'Your report should be headed YouYou not Dada,' he said, after he had read the article. 'Your sentences are filled with a longing for human beings. That is, fundamentally, with a longing for growth, for an extension of one's own little I, for community. So you escape from the loneliness of the sad little I into a world of childish follies. It is a voluntary and therefore enjoyable error. But all the same an error – how can one find another, by losing oneself? But the other – that is, the world in all its magnificent depths – only reveals itself in quietness. But the only way you can find peace is to raise your fingers in accusation: "You, you!"'

I burnt the manuscript.

*

I wrote an article about Oskar Baum's novel, *The Door to the Impossible*.

Franz Kafka gave it to Felix Weltsch, who published it as a middle in the periodical *Self-Defence*. A few days later in Kafka's office I encountered an official – I think his name was Gutling – who immediately began to analyse my article.

His criticism was, of course, hostile.

My review, together with Baum's novel were – in the speaker's eyes – 'dadaist revelations of a diseased mind'.

I said nothing.

When, however, he repeated his assertion for about the fifteenth time, Kafka intervened:

'If Dada is diseased, even then it is only an outward symptom, nothing else. But you will not abolish the disease by isolating and suppressing the symptom. On the contrary, it will only become worse. A single abscess that breaks internally is far more dangerous than several surface abscesses. If there is to be a genuine improvement, you must go to the root of the diseased condition. Only then will the disfigurements resulting from the disorder disappear.'

Gutling did not reply.

The arrival of another official ended our discussion.

When I was alone again with Kafka in the office, I asked: 'Do you also think that my essay on Baum's book was dadaist?'

Kafka smiled.

'Why do you ask? Your essay wasn't even discussed.'

'But please . . .'

Kafka made a contemptuous gesture with his hand.

'That isn't criticism! The critic brandished the word "Dada" as a small child waves a toy sword. He wants to dazzle you with the terrible weapon, because he knows very well that in fact it is only a toy. It is enough to face him with a real sabre for the child to calm down, because he is afraid for his toy.'

'So you were not talking about Baum, and what I had written, but about Dada?'

'Yes, I girded on my sword.'

'But you also regard Dada as a mark of disease,' I said.

'Dada is – a crime,' said Franz Kafka very seriously. 'The spine of the soul has been broken. Faith has collapsed.'

'What is faith?'

'Whoever has faith cannot define it, and whoever has none can only give a definition which lies under the shadow of grace withheld. The man of faith cannot speak and the man of no faith ought not to speak. And in fact the prophets always talk of the levers of faith and never of faith alone.'

'They are the voice of a faith which is silent about itself.'

'Yes, that is so.'

'And Christ?'

Kafka bowed his head.

'He is an abyss filled with light. One must close one's eyes if one is not to fall into it. Max Brod is writing a long work called *Paganism, Christianity, Jewry*.[75] Perhaps in argument with the book I may clarify my own mind a little.'

'Do you expect so much of the book?'

'Not only from the book, but most of all from every single moment. I try to be a true attendant upon grace. Perhaps it will come – perhaps it will not come. Perhaps this quiet yet unquiet waiting is the harbinger of grace, or perhaps it is grace itself. I do not know. But that does not disturb me. In the meantime I – have made friends with my ignorance.'

*

We fell into conversation about the worth and worthlessness of the different confessions.

I tried to obtain a personal declaration from Kafka; but I did not succeed.

Franz Kafka said, 'God can only be comprehended personally. Each man has his own life and his own God. His protector and judge. Priests and rituals are only crutches for the crippled life of the soul.'

*

When Kafka saw a crime novel among the books in my brief-case, he said:

'There is no need to be ashamed of reading such things. Dostoevski's *Crime and Punishment* is after all only a crime novel. And Shakespeare's *Hamlet*? It is a detective story. At the heart of the action is a mystery, which is gradually brought to light. But is there a greater mystery than the truth? Poetry is always an expedition in search of truth.'

'But what is truth?'

Kafka was silent, then gave a sly smile.

'That sounds as if you had caught me out in an empty phrase.

In fact, it is not so. Truth is what every man needs in order to live, but can obtain or purchase from no one. Each man must reproduce it for himself from within, otherwise he must perish. Life without truth is not possible. Truth is perhaps life itself.'

*

Kafka gave me an inch-thick volume published by the *Reklam Verlag*: the American Walt Whitman's book of poems, *Leaves of Grass*.

He said to me: 'The translation is not particularly good. In some places even it's very clumsy. Yet it gives one at least an approximate idea of the poet, who belongs among the greatest formal innovators in the modern lyric. One can regard his unrhymed verse as the progenitor of the free rhythms of Arno Holz, Emile Verhaeren, and Paul Claudel, as well as of the Czech poet Stanislav Kostka, Neumann and others.'

I hastened to remark that Jaroslav Vrchlický, who – according to official Czech literary criticism – 'opened the windows of the world to Czech literature', had also translated Whitman's *Leaves of Grass* some years ago as a linguistic experiment.

'I know,' said Kafka. 'The formal element in Walt Whitman's poetry found an enormous echo throughout the world. Yet Walt Whitman's significance lies elsewhere. He combined the contemplation of nature and of civilization, which are apparently entirely contradictory, into a single intoxicating vision of life, because he always had sight of the transitoriness of all phenomena. He said: "Living is the little that is left over from dying." So he gave his whole heart to every leaf of grass. I admire in him the reconciliation of art and nature. When the war between the Northern and Southern States in America, which first really set in motion the power of our present machine world, first broke out, Walt Whitman became a medical orderly. He did then what all of us ought to do, particularly today. He helped the weak, the sick and the defeated. He was really a Christian and – with a close affinity especially to us Jews – he was therefore an important measure of the status and worth of humanity.'

'So you know his work very well?'

'Not so much his work as his life. For that after all is his real masterpiece. What he wrote, his poems and essays, are only the flickering embers of the fire of a faith consistently and actively lived.'

*

I showed Franz Kafka the German translation of Oscar Wilde's essays, *Intentions*,[76] which Leo Lederer had given me.

Kafka turned the leaves and said:

'It sparkles and seduces, as only a poison can sparkle and seduce.'

'Do you not like the book?'

'I did not say that. On the contrary: one could like it only too easily. And that is one of the book's great dangers. For it is dangerous, because it plays with truth. A game with truth is always a game with life.'

'Do you mean then that without truth there is no real life?'

Franz Kafka nodded in silence.

After a short pause he said:

'A lie is often an expression of the fear that one may be crushed by the truth. It is a projection of one's own littleness, of the sin of which one is afraid.'

*

'I am completely ineffective as an administrator,' lamented Kafka once when I met him in his office as he stood behind his desk with a despairing face. 'I can never finally dispose of any case. With me, everything remains in suspense.'

'I don't see any sign of it,' I said. 'Your desk is clean.'

'That's just it,' Kafka replied, and sat down. 'I pass every document on as quickly as I can. But that doesn't put an end to it for me. I follow it in my thoughts. From one department to another, from desk to desk, through the chain of hands it passes through before it reaches its final destination. My imagination is always breaking out of the four walls of my office. But that doesn't make my horizon any wider. On the contrary, it contracts. And I with it.' He smiled painfully. 'I'm just a bit of waste matter and not even that. I don't fall under the wheels, but only into the cogs of the machine, a mere nothing in the glutinous bureaucracy of the Accident Insurance Institution.'

I interrupted him: 'In short, office life is – as my father says – a dog's life.'

'Yes,' Kafka agreed. 'Yet I don't bark at anyone and I don't bite either. As you know – I'm a vegetarian. We only live on our own flesh.'

We both laughed so loud that we nearly didn't hear the knock on the door of a colleague who was about to enter.

*

I told him that my father and I had visited the Franciscan monastery near the Wenzelsplatz in Prague.

Franz Kafka said, 'It is a family community based on choice. Man voluntarily limits his own self, surrenders his highest and most real property, his own person, in order to find salvation. By outward restraint he tries to achieve inner freedom. That is the meaning of self-submission to the Law.'

'But if a man does not know the Law,' I said, 'how will he achieve freedom?'

'He will have the Law beaten into him. If he does not know the Law, he will be harried and whipped into knowledge.'

'So you mean that sooner or later every man must arrive at true knowledge.'

'I did not quite say that. I did not speak of knowledge, but of freedom as a goal. The knowledge is only a way . . .'

'To fulfilment? Then life is only a task, a commission.'

Kafka made a helpless gesture.

'That is just it. Man cannot see beyond himself. He is in the dark.'

*

Once when I called on Kafka he was standing at the window with my father. They turned around, but only acknowledged my greeting with a brief nod of the head. Immediately afterwards, Kafka asked my father, 'So during the short time you served in the war, you found that the soldiers were relatively better off than civilians?'

'Yes,' said my father. 'In the army there wasn't as great a food shortage as in civilian life. We always had bread. The soldiers were better cared for than civilians.'

'That's understandable,' said Kafka, and reflectively rubbed his smoothly shaven cheek. 'Money had been spent on the soldiers. They represented an investment by the state, which had to be protected. They were specialists. On the other hand, the civilians were only human beings, in whom the state took as little interest as possible.'

'Yes,' sighed my father. 'One could see that with frightening clarity in the typhus barracks. Thank God, that horror is over.'

'It's not over,' said Kafka quietly, and went to his desk where he stood with bent head. 'The horror is only collecting its strength to break out again under more favourable circumstances.'

'You think there'll be another war?' said my father, opening his eyes in alarm.

But Kafka said nothing.

'That's impossible!' cried my father, waving his arms excitedly. 'There cannot be another war.'

'Why not?' said Kafka tonelessly, looking my father straight in the eye. 'You're only expressing a wish. Or can you say with complete conviction that this war was the last war?'

My father was silent. I could see how his eyelids twitched.

Kafka sat down, locked his bony fingers together on his desk, and took a deep breath.

'No, I cannot say that,' my father said at last. 'You're right. It is only a wish.'

'Such a wish is natural, when one's sunk up to one's neck in a bog,' replied Kafka, without looking at my father. 'We live in a period of human inflation. Men profit by destroying civilians, who are cheaper than soldiers and cannon.'

'But all the same!' my father declared, 'I don't believe in another war. The majority of men are against it.'

'That has nothing to do with it,' said Kafka in a resigned voice. 'Majorities decide nothing. They always do what they are told. Decisions are made by the individuals who go against the stream. But such individuals no longer exist. They have liquidated themselves by their own demand for comfort. *Kosile bližší nežli kabát. Tím zajdeme ve vlastní špíne.* (The shirt sticks closer to one than the jacket. Thereby we shall perish in our own dirt.) We shall all perish miserably, unless every single one of us immediately throws away his own moral dirty washing.'

*

Franz Kafka was the first person who took my spiritual life seriously, who talked to me like an adult and so strengthened my self-confidence. His interest in me was a wonderful gift to me. I was always conscious of this. Once I even expressed myself in this sense to him.

'Do I not waste your time? I am so stupid. You give me so much and I give you nothing.'

Kafka was plainly embarrassed by my words.

'Now, now,' he said soothingly. 'You are a child. You are not a robber. I do indeed give you my time, but it belongs not to me but to the Workmen's Accident Insurance Institution; both of us conspire to rob it of my time. After all, that is splendid! Also you are not stupid. So stop using such phrases, by which you only force me to admit that I enjoy your youthful devotion and understanding.'

*

A walk on the Quay.

I told Kafka that I had been ill, had been in bed with influenza and worked at a play, called *Saul*.

Kafka took great interest in this literary venture, for which I wished to employ a three-storied stage. Three platforms, one above the other, were to represent three spiritual worlds: on the ground floor, the Street, or forum of the People; above it the King's Palace, or the house of the individual; and, yet above, the Temple of the spiritual-temporal power, through which the voice of the unseen speaks.

'So the whole is a pyramid, whose apex loses itself in the clouds,' said Franz Kafka. 'And the centre of gravity? Where is the centre of gravity in the world of your play?'

'Underneath, in the mass basis of the people,' I answered. 'In spite of a few individual characters, it is a play about the anonymous crowd.'

Franz Kafka contracted his heavy eyebrows, slightly protruded his under lip, moistened his lips with the tip of his tongue, and without looking at me said:

'I think that you start from false premises. Anonymous means the same as nameless. The Jewish people, however, has never been nameless. On the contrary, it is the chosen race of a personal God which can never sink to the mean level of an anonymous and therefore soulless mass, as long as it can hold fast to the fulfilment of the Law. Mankind can only become a grey, formless, and therefore nameless mass through a fall from the Law which gives it form. But in that case there is no above and below any more; life is levelled out into mere existence; there is no struggle, no drama, only the consumption of matter, decay. But that is not the world of the Bible and of Jewry.'

I defended myself.

'For me it isn't a matter of Jewry and the Bible. The biblical material is for me only a means to presenting the masses of today.'

Kafka shook his head.

'Exactly! What you are aiming at is false. You cannot turn life into an allegory of death. That would be sinful.'

'What do you mean by sin?'

'Sin is turning away from one's own vocation, misunderstanding, impatience, and sloth - that is sin. The poet has the task of leading the isolated and mortal into eternal life, the accidental into conformity to law. He has a prophetic task.'

'Then to write means to lead,' I said.

'The true word leads; the untrue misleads,' said Kafka. 'It is not an accident that the Bible is called Writ. It is the voice of the Jewish people, which does not belong to an historic yesterday, but is completely contemporary. In your play you treat it as if it were an historically mummified fact, and that is false. If I understand you rightly, you wish to bring the modern masses on to the stage. They have nothing in common with the Bible. That is the heart of your play. The people of the Bible is an association of individuals by means of a Law. But the masses of today resist every form of association. They split apart by reason of their own lawlessness. That is the motive power of their perpetual movement. The masses hurry, run, march in thunder through our era. Where to? Where have they come from? No one knows. The more they march, the less they achieve their goal. They use their strength to no purpose. They think they are on the move. And thus, marking time, they fall into the void. That is all. Mankind has lost its home.'

'Then how do you explain the growth of nationalism?' I asked.

'That is precisely the proof of what I say,' answered Franz Kafka. 'Men always strive for what they do not have. The technical advances which are common to all nations strip them more and more of their national characteristics. Therefore they become nationalist. Modern nationalism is a defensive movement against the crude encroachments of civilization. One sees that best in the case of the Jews. If they felt at home in their environment and could easily come to terms with it, there would be no Zionism. But the pressure of our environment makes us see our own features. We are going home. To our roots.'

'And are you then convinced that Zionism is the only right road?'

Kafka gave an embarrassed smile.

'One only knows the rightness or wrongness of the road when one has reached the goal. At least now we are going.

We are on the move, and so we live. Around us anti-semitism increases, but that is all to the good. The Talmud says that we Jews only yield our best, like olives, when we are crushed.'

'I believe that the progressive labour movement will not permit any further growth of anti-semitism,' I said.

But Franz Kafka only bowed his head sadly.

'You are mistaken. I believe that anti-semitism will also seize hold of the masses. One can see that happening in the Workmen's Accident Insurance Institution. It is a creation of the labour movement. It should therefore be filled with the radiant spirit of progress. But what happens? The Institution is a dark nest of bureaucrats, in which I function as the solitary display-Jew.'

'That is wretched,' I said.

'Yes, man is wretched, because amid the continually increasing masses he becomes minute by minute more isolated.'

*

We talked about smoking.

I said: 'Most of the boys I know began to smoke in order to look grown up in their own eyes. I was never taken in by such nonsense.'

'You have your father to thank for that,' said Kafka.

'Yes,' I agreed. 'One can – like my father – be a grown man without copying the stupidities of grown men.'

'On the contrary!' declared Kafka, waving his hand in the air. 'Anyone who allows himself to be led and dictated to by the bad habits and opinions of his surroundings has no respect for himself. But without self-respect there's no morality, no order, no continuity, no life-giving warmth. So a man decays like a bit of shapeless cow-dung. He has no value except to horse flies and other insects.'

*

With Franz Kafka in his office.

He sat tired behind his desk. His arms hanging down. Lips tightly pressed. Smiling, he stretched out his hand to me.

'I had a terribly bad night.'

'Have you been to the doctor?'

He pursed his mouth.

'The doctor . . .'

He raised his left-hand palm upward, then let it fall.

'One cannot escape oneself. That is fate. The only possibility is to look on and forget that a game is being played with us.'

*

Frau Svátek, who lived in the Jeseniusgasse in Žižkov, used to work as a servant in my father's house in the mornings. In the afternoons she worked as a charwoman in the Workmen's Accident Insurance Institution. She saw me several times with Franz Kafka, whom she knew, and so one day she began to talk about him to me.

'Kafka is a fine man. He is quite different from the others. You can see that even in the way he gives you something. The others hand it to you in such a way that it almost burns you to take it. They don't give – they humiliate and insult you. One would often like to throw their tips away. But Kafka gives, really gives, in such a way that it's a pleasure. For instance, a bunch of grapes which he has not eaten that morning. They are left-overs. You know what they usually look like – with most people. But Kafka never leaves them looking like a tasteless lump. He leaves the grapes or the fruit nicely arranged on the plate. And when I come into the office, he says, by the way, could I possibly make use of them. Yes, Kafka does not treat me like an old char. He is a fine man.'

Frau Svátek was right. Kafka had the art of giving. He never said, 'Take this, it is a present.' When he gave a book or a magazine, all he ever said was, 'There is no need to give it me back.'

*

We talked about N. I said that N. was stupid. Kafka replied:

'To be stupid is human. Many clever people are not wise,

and therefore in the last resort not even clever. They are merely inhuman out of fear of their own meaningless vulgarity.'

*

With Kafka was an official who had a rather tough manner of speaking.

'What sort of a man is that?' I asked, when we were alone in the office.

'That is N.,' said Kafka.

'A brute,' I said.

'Why? He merely follows a different kind of convention. Probably he has learned that good manners make silk purses out of sows' ears, so he prefers to wear homespun instead of a frock coat. That's all it is.'

*

On Kafka's desk lay a pile of letters, pictures and travel brochures.

To my look of inquiry he replied that he wished to spend some time in a small mountain sanatorium.

'I don't want to go into a health factory,' he said. 'All I want is some kind of family *pension*, where one will be under medical care. I don't want any comforts or invalid luxury.'

I said: 'The most important thing for you is the location and the mountain air.'

'Yes, that as well,' Kafka agreed. 'But the most valuable thing is that one should be forced, even for a short time, to cast off the chains of one's old habits – to present, in the show window of the world that has been clarified by memory, an inventory of the much depleted portfolio of one's life. Wherever one goes, one only travels towards one's own misunderstood nature.'

*

A damp autumn, and a surprisingly hard and early winter made Kafka's illness worse.

His desk in the office stood empty and abandoned.

'He is feverish,' said Treml, who sat at the other desk. 'Perhaps we shall not see him again.'

I went sadly home.

But one day Franz Kafka was in the office again.

Pale, stooping, smiling.

In a tired, gentle voice he told me he had only come to hand over some documents and to fetch various personal papers from his desk. He said he was not well. In the next few days he was going to the High Tatra. To a sanatorium.

'That's good,' I said. 'Go as quickly as possible – if it is possible.'

Franz Kafka smiled sadly.

'That is precisely what is irritating and difficult. Life has so many possibilities, and each one only mirrors the inescapable impossibility of one's own existence.'

His voice broke into a dry convulsive cough, which he quickly mastered.

We smiled at each other.

'Look,' I said, 'everything will soon be all right.'

'It is already all right,' Franz Kafka said slowly. 'I have said yes to everything. In that way suffering becomes an enchantment, and death – it is only an ingredient in the sweetness of life.'

*

At parting before his journey to the sanatorium in the Tatra I said:

'You will recover and come back in good health. The future will make up for everything. Everything will change.'

Kafka, smiling, laid the index finger of his right hand on his chest.

'The future is already here within me. The only change will be to make visible the hidden wounds.'

I became impatient.

'If you do not believe in a cure, why are you going to the sanatorium?'

Kafka bowed over his writing-table.

'The accused always endeavours to secure a postponement of sentence.'

*

With my friend Helene Slaviček I returned from Chlumetz to Prague. We went to my father in his office, to announce our arrival. On the stairs we met Franz Kafka. I introduced him to Helene. Two days later he said to me:

'Women are snares, which lie in wait for men on all sides in order to drag them into the merely finite. They lose their dangers if one voluntarily falls into one of the snares. But if, as a result of habit, one overcomes it, then all the jaws of the female trap open again.'

*

When I met Kafka alone in the Accident Insurance Institution the day after my visit with Helene Slaviček, I asked him: 'What did you think of Helene?'

He leaned his head to his left shoulder and said: 'That is entirely unimportant. She is your girlfriend. You must be enchanted. In love – as in all forms of enchantment – everything depends on one single word. The extensive, undefined phrase *a* woman must be replaced by the precisely defined phrase, *the* woman. A generic concept must become a force of destiny. Then all is in order.'

*

Talking about the leading personalities of the Prague Association, *Poale Zion*, we came to discuss the ex-actor Rudolf K., undoubtedly the group's best orator. I referred to the successes which 'the beautiful Rudi' had with women. Kafka said: 'A man's good luck in such matters is for women a misfortune which lays waste their lives. It's a great offence, a crime, like every one-sided piece of luck extracted out of misfortune and need. A man who suns himself in so false a form of good luck will end somewhere in some abandoned corner suffocating from his own fear and egotism.'

*

The young F.W. committed suicide because of an unhappy love affair.

We discussed the case.

Franz Kafka said during our conversation:

'What is love? After all, it is quite simple. Love is everything which enhances, widens, and enriches our life. In its heights and in its depths. Love has as few problems as a motor-car. The only problems are the driver, the passengers, and the road.'

*

I told him about my school friend W., who when ten years old was seduced by his French governess and afterwards was afraid of all young girls, even his own sister, so that now he was under the medical attention of Doktor Pötzl, the psychoanalyst.

'Love always inflicts wounds which never heal, because love always appears hand in hand with filth,' said Kafka. 'Only the will of the loved one can divide the love from the filth. But someone as helpless as your young friend has no will of his own, and so he is infected by the filth. He is a victim to the bewilderment of adolescence. Such things can cause grave damage. A man's embittered features are often only the petrified bewilderment of a boy.'

*

Once when, during a walk, I talked about my friend Helene S., Franz Kafka said:

'In the moment of love a man is responsible not only to himself but to all other men. Yet at the same time he finds himself in a state of intoxication which impairs his powers of judgement. The content of the human I is then greater than the narrow field of vision of his immediate consciousness. Consciousness is only a part of the I. Yet every decision gives a new direction to the I. In this way the commonest and most difficult conflicts arise, through misunderstanding.'

*

In conversation about C., Kafka said:

'The root of the word sensuous is sense. This has a perfectly definite significance. One can achieve sense only through the senses. Of course, this path like every other has its dangers. One may prefer the means to the end. In this way one might end up in sensuality, which tends to distract one's attention from sense.'

*

I remember that I used to notice that Franz Kafka had a great liking for ironic puns and verbal tricks of a very personal kind. Yet in my notes I can find only one example.

I had told him that in the fourth form of my secondary school there used to be an active business in lending out copies of Otto Julius Bierbaum's novel, *Prince Kuckuck*.

'It was the description of his debauches that attracted us,' I said.

'Wastrel,' said Kafka. 'For me the word always conjures up the idea of a waste land, of abandonment. The wastrel is abandoned in the waste.'

'Woman is the waste,' I said.

Franz Kafka shrugged his shoulders.

'Perhaps. The well of pleasure is the well of his loneliness. The more he drinks, the more sober he becomes. In the end he can no longer quench his thirst. So he goes on drinking, but his thirst is never satiated. That is what a wastrel is.'

*

Opposite the old building of the Workmen's Accident Insurance Institution on the Pořič was an old hotel painted a golden brown, *Zum goldenen Fasan*. It was a one-storied house frequented mostly by the women who paraded to and fro in front of the hotel. Once when I had been waiting for Kafka in front of the Insurance office, he said:

'I saw from up above how intensely you were eyeing the girls parading. So I hurried.'

I felt myself blushing, so I said:

'The women don't interest me. As a matter of fact, I am only interested in - in their customers.'

Kafka gave me a sidelong glance, looked straight ahead, and after a while said:

'The Czech language is wonderfully penetrating and precise. The term "will o' the wisp" (*bludcika*) for this kind of women is wonderfully true. How wretched, abandoned, frozen men must be, when they wish to warm themselves by these marsh gases! They must be so miserable and so lost that any inquisitive glance might hurt them. So one ought not to watch them. Yet if one turned one's head away, they might take it as a sign of contempt. It is difficult . . . The road to love always goes through filth and misery. Yet if one despised the road one might easily miss the goal. Therefore one must humbly suffer the various misadventures of the road. Only thus will one reach one's goal – perhaps.'

*

When once I found Kafka in his office studying various Czech legal regulations, with a mocking look in his eyes he swept them with a disdainful gesture into the open drawer of his desk.

I said: 'They must be boring to read, mustn't they?'

'Not so much boring as repellent,' Kafka replied. 'To the legislator, men are all criminals and cowards, who can only be governed by legal threats and fear. That is not only false but it is also very short-sighted and therefore – especially for the legislator – very dangerous.'

'Why for the legislator?'

'Because men's inner selves escape them. As a result of his contempt for human beings, the legislator produces, instead of order, a more or less visible form of anarchy.'

'I don't understand you very well.'

'Yet it's very simple,' said Kafka, and leaned back comfortably in his chair. 'Owing to the continuous technical transformation of the world, more and more individuals are being compressed into a human mass. The character of any mass, however, depends on the structure and the internal motion of its smallest parts. That is also true of men in the wars. Therefore one must stimulate every single individual by the trust one places in him, one must give him self-respect and hope and, through them, real freedom. Only so can we work and live and not feel the apparatus of the law which encompasses us as a degrading constraint.'

*

During the period of my visits to Franz Kafka in the office on the Poříč, my parents' marriage had been going through a severe crisis. I suffered because of the domestic quarrels. I complained of this to Kafka and admitted that the troubles around me were the decisive motive for my literary efforts.

'If things were different at home, perhaps I would not write at all,' I said. 'I want to escape the unrest, to shut out the voices around me and within me, and so I write. Just as some people make silly objects with a fret-saw in order to get through the boredom of their evenings at home, so I patch words and sentences and paragraphs together, to have an excuse for being alone and to cut myself off from my surroundings, which suffocate me.'

'You are quite right,' said Kafka. 'Many men do the same. In one of his letters Flaubert writes that his novel is a rock to which he clings in order not to be drowned in the waves of the world around him.'

'Well, I am a Gustav too, but not a Flaubert,' I said, smiling.

'The technique of spiritual hygiene is not reserved for rare individuals. So that Flaubert's name will not embarrass you, I will confess that at a certain period I did exactly as you are doing. Only in my case things were a little more complicated. By scribbling I run ahead of myself in order to catch myself up at the finishing post. I cannot run away from myself.'

*

The trouble between my parents was reflected in my conversations with Franz Kafka.

'I cannot bear what is called family life,' I said.

'That is wrong,' said Kafka, with unspoken sympathy. 'How would it be if you were merely to observe the life of your family? The family would think that you were sharing their life and were content. And in fact this would be partly true. You would be living with your family, but on different terms from them. That would be all. You would be outside the circle, with your face turned inwards towards the family, and that would be enough. Perhaps now and then you might even see your own image reflected in your family's eyes – quite small and as if drawn on a glass ball in the garden.'

'What you propose is a pure course of spiritual acrobatics,' I said.

'Quite right,' Kafka nodded. 'They are the acrobatics of everyday. They are dangerous, because normally one is not conscious of them. Yet they may break, not one's neck, but the soul itself. One does not die of it, but continues to exist as one of life's deserving pensioners.'

'Who, for example?'

'No one. One can only give examples of exceptions. But so called reasonable people are usually those who have been disabled by life. And they are the dominant majority, and do not tolerate examples which reflect unfavourably on themselves.'

*

Once when I was again complaining about the quarrels in my family, Kafka said:

'Do not excite yourself. Be calm. Quietness is indeed a sign of strength. But quietness may also help one to achieve strength. That is the law of opposites. So be quiet. Calmness and quietness make one free – even on the scaffold.'

*

At home, matters developed into a total rupture. My mother persecuted my father with jealous reproaches which grew louder and louder. Beside her over-fourteen-year-younger husband she felt worn out and old. This gave her a sense of inferiority which she only succeeded in increasing by her condemnation of her partner in marriage. She suspected him of unfaithfulness and since she could find no objective evidence of it, she attributed to him immense cunning and powers of deception. This expressed itself in looks of hate, words of hostility and in small but increasing demonstrations of contempt.

Meals were not properly prepared. Father's favourite dishes vanished from the table; the house was untidy when father returned from the office; the curtains flapped in the open windows; a bucket full of dirty water stood on the table in the kitchen; beds and mattresses were piled in disorder in the bedrooms; the lady of the house was out and the maid had been given an extra day off. Father stood bewildered in an alien and unpleasant world. At first this led to half-suppressed grumbling and then to verbal battles that became increasingly louder and more violent.

After one such scene which – with a short intermission for the necessary night's sleep – lasted from the afternoon of one day until dawn and early morning of the next, I went to Kafka completely shattered by shame, anger and hopelessness. He listened quietly to the account I stammered out in my agitation. Then he locked his desk, put the key in his pocket and said: 'Do you know what? I'll forget about the office and you forget the things that are oppressing you. We'll play a duet together and go for a walk. Musíme se vyluftovat (We need some air).'

Outside the building he put a hand under my arm and said with a smile: 'We'll make a tour of the former royal capital. Respectable idlers usually start by taking a glass of wine or brandy together. Unfortunately, neither of us is satisfied with such a modest form of dissipation. We need more sophisticated opiates. So we will go to Andrée.'

'I only have a few krone on me,' I said plaintively.

'Me too,' said Kafka, with a frivolous wave of the hand. 'But I know a certain Herr Demi; he'll look after us.'

Kafka was not mistaken. Herr Demi, by birth from Rostock,

had fallen in love with Prague, and as an expert in his profession had quickly made an excellent reputation in the bookselling trade; on the black sales counter of his shop near the Pulverturm he displayed an enormous variety of new and second-hand books. I do not remember what Herr Demi showed us that day. I only remember what Kafka bought for me and for himself, and what he said about each book.

For me Kafka bought *David Copperfield* by Charles Dickens, *Before and After* by Paul Gauguin, and Arthur Rimbaud's *Life and Poetry*. The Dickens I chose myself, it was one of the few of this writer's books which was missing from my library.

Kafka approved my choice.

He said: 'Dickens is one of my favourite authors. Yes, for a time indeed he was the model for what I vainly aimed at. Your beloved Karl Rossman is a distant relation of David Copperfield and Oliver Twist.'[78]

'What do you find attractive in Dickens . . . ?'

Kafka replied without any pause for reflection: 'His mastery of the material world. His balance between the external and the internal. His masterly and yet completely unaffected representation of the interaction between the world and the I. The perfectly natural proportions of his work. They are lacking in most of the painters and writers of today. You realize that, for instance, in these two Frenchmen.'

And he forcibly pressed upon me the two above-named books by Gauguin and Rimbaud.

For himself he bought three volumes of Gustave Flaubert's *Journal*. As he did so, he said: 'Flaubert's diaries are very important and very interesting. I have owned them for a long time. Now I'm buying them again for Oskar Baum.'

I wanted to carry both parcels of books but Kafka would not let me. 'Ne, ne! To nyde (No, no! That won't do). You must not carry my means of debauch. One can't let anyone else play one's part for one in intoxication or in death.'

I disagreed. 'Since you've bought the books for Baum, they can't be the means of intoxication for you. So I can carry them.'

But Kafka shook his head violently. 'No, no! That won't do. My form of drunkenness lies precisely in giving. It's the most refined form of drunkenness that exists. I won't have it diminished by being helped.'

So we walked side by side, each with his parcel of books under his arm, across the Graben and along the Wenzelsplatz, left at the equestrian statue of Saint Wenceslas and right past the New German Theater into the municipal park, drank a glass of milk each at the little kiosk on the edge of the Bredauergasse, paused a moment at the little duckpool with its plashing artificial waterfall, went round it by a steeply sloping path to the tram stop and returned by tram to the Ring.

On the way, Kafka talked about the authors of the other books he had bought for me in addition to *David Copperfield*.

He said: 'The tension between the subjective world of the I, and the objective external world, is the fundamental problem of all art. Every painter, writer, dramatist and fabricator of verses must come to terms with it. In doing so, naturally, he achieves the most varied combinations of the materials which lie to hand. For the painter Paul Gauguin, reality is a flying trapeze act performed with absolutely individual tricks of form and colour. Rimbaud does the same thing with language. Yes, Rimbaud even goes beyond words. He transforms vowels into colours. By this wizardry of sound and colour he comes near to the magical religious practices of primitive races. They kneel down, penetrated by fear and awe, before various idols of wood and stone. Progress, however, has depreciated the value of material things. So we make ourselves into idols. For that reason, we are even more harshly and deeply bound and beaten by the shadow of fear.'

Kafka looked reflectively out of the window.

Later I tried to return to this subject of modern idolatry which he had raised – but to no effect. Kafka did not respond to the suggestions and questions I put to him on the subject.

We left the tram on the north side of the Hradschin, walked a little way along the Marienschanze and the Staubbrücke, through two courtyards of the Burg, past the Schwedische

Palais and the Aussichtsrampe, up the steps of the old Rathaus into the Lorettogasse and to the Lorettoplatz, where we again took the tram as Kafka was tired.

At the Altstädter Ring, not far from his house, he said to me: 'The trouble in your home, of which you have told me, doesn't affect you only. Your parents are even more distressed and humiliated by it. Your parents, because of the estrangement which has torn them apart, have lost much of the most valuable thing which human beings can possess, and of their lives and the meaning of life. So your parents – in any case, like most people in our time – have been spiritually crippled. People today are for the most part mutilated in their sensibility and their imagination. You should therefore not reject your parents. On the contrary! You must guide and support them like the halt and the blind.'

'How can I do that?' I said despairingly.

'By your love.'

'When both of them attack me?'

'Yes, especially then. By your calm, your care and patience, in short – through your love, you must revive in your parents what is already dying in both of them. You must love them in spite of every blow and every injustice and lead them to justice and self-respect. For what is in-justice. A false judgement, an error and a fall, a crawling in the dust, a posture unworthy of a human being. You must raise your parents and put them to rights by your love, as if they were both out of their minds. That is what you must do. Like all of us. Otherwise, we are not human. You must not condemn them because of your own pain.'

His hand hovered lightly over my left cheek.

'Good night, Gusti.'

Kafka turned around and disappeared behind the dark glass door of his house.

I stood as if paralysed.

He had said *Gusti*, like my parents, and his hand . . .

I still felt the light and gentle touch of his fingertips. Yet I felt a shiver up my backbone, I could not help sneezing, as if

I had caught a cold, and my chin trembled as I strode straight across the Altstädter Ring to the dark Eisengasse.

*

I told Kafka that my father would not allow me to study music.

'And are you going to submit to your father's command?' Kafka asked.

'Why should I?' I answered. 'I have a head of my own.'

Kafka looked at me very seriously.

'Using one's own head is often the easiest way of losing it,' he said. 'Of course, I am not saying anything against your studying music. On the contrary! The only strong and deep passions are those which can stand the test of reason.'

'Music is not a passion but an art,' I said.

But Franz Kafka smiled.

'There is passion behind every art. That is why you fight and suffer for your music. That is why you do not submit to your father's orders, because you love music and all that it implies more than your own parents. But in art that is always the way. One must throw one's life away in order to gain it.'

*

When the quarrel between my parents had reached the stage of divorce proceedings, I told Kafka that I was going to leave home.

Franz Kafka slowly nodded.

'That is painful. But it is the best one can do in such circumstances. There are some things one can only achieve by a deliberate leap in the opposite direction. One has to go abroad in order to find the home one has lost.'

When I told him that I would work as a musician at night, he said:

'That is very bad for one's health. And besides you tear yourself out of the human community. The night-side of life becomes its day-side for you, and what is day for other men changes into a dream. Without noticing it, you have emigrated to the antipodes of the world around you. Now, when you are young, you will not notice anything wrong, but later, in a few years' time, you will shut your eyes in horror before the void within you. You will lose the power of vision, and the waves of the world will close over your head.'

*

After the first hearing of my parents' divorce case, I visited Franz Kafka.

I was very distraught, filled with pain and therefore – unjust. When I had exhausted my complaints, Kafka said to me:

'Just be quiet and patient. Let evil and unpleasantness pass quietly over you. Do not try to avoid them. On the contrary, observe them carefully. Let active understanding take the place of reflex irritation, and you will grow out of your trouble. Men can achieve greatness only by surmounting their own littleness.'

*

'Patience is the master key to every situation. One must have sympathy for everything, surrender to everything, but at the same time remain patient and forbearing,' Kafka said to me, when we were walking one crystalline autumn day through the leafless Baumgarten. 'There is no such thing as bending or breaking. It's a question only of overcoming, which begins with overcoming oneself. That cannot be avoided. To abandon that path is always to break in pieces. One must patiently accept everything and let it grow within oneself. The barriers of the fear-ridden I can only be broken by love. One must, in the dead leaves that rustle around one, already see the young fresh green of spring, compose oneself in patience, and wait. Patience is the only true foundation on which to make one's dreams come true.'

This was Kafka's fundamental principle in life, and he tried to impress it on me with never-failing understanding. It was a principle, of whose truth he convinced me by his every word and gesture, every smile and every look of his large eyes, and

by all his long years of service in the Accident Insurance
Institution.

As I learned from my father, for fourteen years, that is to
say for nearly half the average length of a generation, Franz
Kafka sat behind his smoothly polished desk in the smoke-
fumed air of the factory at No. 7 on the Pořič. He entered the
Institution on 30 July 1908, as an assistant and at his own
request retired as a principal secretary on 1 July 1922. Frau
Svátek, who cleaned Kafka's office, and also our own house in
Karolinenthal, told me: 'Kafka came and went as silently as a
mouse. He disappeared in the same way as he lived at the
Insurance Institution throughout the years. I don't know who
cleared out his desk. In his hanging cupboard there was only
Kafka's threadbare grey second-best coat which he kept there
for a rainy day. I've never seen him with an umbrella. A cleaner
took his coat. Whether he took it to Kafka or kept it – I don't
know. I scrubbed the empty cupboard with soap and water.
On his desk stood an old, slender glass vase, containing two
pencils and a penholder. Next to it was a lovely blue-and-gold
teacup and a saucer to match. Treml, who watched me while
I cleaned up, said: "Take that rubbish away!" The vase was
part of Kafka's working equipment. He often drank milk and
sometimes tea out of the cup. So I took what Treml called the
rubbish and brought it home.'

I was sitting opposite her in the kitchen. Frau Svátek went
to a white glass-fronted china cupboard, from which she took
the 'rubbish' rejected by Treml, cleaned them carefully with a
cloth and respectfully placed them before me on the table.

'Take them, young man. You were very fond of Kafka. I
know that. You don't have to tell me. He was very good to you
when you really needed it. I'm sure you will take good care of
the cup he used to drink from.'

And so indeed I did. The little porcelain cup accompanied
me in the most varied circumstances and dwellings. But I never
used it. I was ashamed to put my lips to the rim which Kafka
had raised to his mouth.

Whenever I saw the blue-and-gold cup which Frau Svátek

had given me, I could not help thinking of the words which Kafka once spoke to me in the twilight as we were walking through the rainswept Teinhof: 'Life is as infinitely great and profound as the immensity of the stars above us. One can only look at it through the narrow keyhole of one's own personal existence. But through it one perceives more than one can see. So above all one must keep the keyhole clean.'

Have I always done that?

I don't know; I believe that only a saint – like Kafka – could do it.

*

In the summer of 1924 I was in Obergeorgenthal near Brux. On Friday, 20 June, I repeat Friday, 20 June, I received a letter from a friend in Prague, the painter Erich Hirt.

He wrote, 'I have just learnt from the editorial staff of the *Tagblatt* that the writer Franz Kafka died on 3 June in a small private sanatorium in Kierling near Vienna. He was, however, buried here in Prague on Wednesday, 11 June 1924, in the Jewish cemetery in Straschnitz.'79

I looked at the little picture of my father which hung on the wall over my bed.

On 14 May 1924, he left this life of his own free will.

Twenty-one days later, on 3 June, Kafka died.

Twenty-one days later . . .

Twenty-one days . . .

Twenty-one . . .

Exactly my own age, as the emotional and intellectual horizon of my youth broke up.

POSTSCRIPT:
THE HISTORY OF THIS BOOK

*

The first edition of my notes and reminiscences, which I originally called *Kafka said to Me*, and the publishers, *Conversations with Kafka*, was published in 1951. It immediately aroused great interest among the reading public, and among reviewers, and in the course of years this interest has increased. My little book became a highly regarded source for literary research. The original German edition of *Conversations with Kafka* was quickly followed by Swedish, American, Jugoslav, Spanish, English, and even Japanese translations.

The daily post brought me, from the farthest corners and ends of the earth, a large number of letters and inquiries which I was always glad to answer – as far as I could. I could always leave unanswered any questions which gave me difficulty. But it was not always so simple in the increasing number of interviews with admirers of Kafka from various countries who came to visit me in Prague. I was often reduced to silence because they all knew Kafka's work, especially his novels, far better than I did. For them, *The Trial*, *America*, *The Castle*, were not merely the titles of books, they were the subject of serious study. For me they were not.

It is impossible for me to read the novels and diaries of Franz Kafka. Not because he is alien to me, but because he is far too close. The living Kafka whom I knew was far greater than the posthumously published books, which his friend Max Brod preserved from destruction. The Franz Kafka whom I used to visit and was allowed to accompany on his walks through Prague had such greatness and inner certainty that even today, at every turning point in my life, I can hold fast to the memory of his shade as if it were solidly cast in steel.

I cannot read Franz Kafka's books because I fear that by studying the writings which were first published after his death I might weaken, dissipate or even lose altogether the magic of his personality.

The smiling Franz Kafka, who in the years when I knew him already lived in the shadow of death, awakened me to feeling and to thought. He was spiritually the greatest figure, and also the most powerfully formative character, of my youthful years, a real man who fought for truth and to preserve life, of whose bitter struggle, waged in silence, for human existence I was a witness. The look of his face, his soft voice and loud fits of coughing; the image of his tall, slim figure; the elegant gestures of his gentle hands; the shadows and the brilliance of his large changeable eyes, whose light gave emphasis to his words; something that was imperishable and unique, and that was therefore unrepeatable and eternal, in his personality, in his outer and his inner self; all this vibrates in me like an echo, which reverberates, in an endless series of images, through the corridors and abysses of my days and years, and with time does not die but only stands out in greater and clearer relief.

For me, the author of *The Metamorphosis*, *The Verdict*, of *The Country Doctor*, *In the Penal Settlement* and the *Letters to Milena*, works with which I am familiar, is a prophet of a consistent ethical responsibility for every living thing, a man in whose apparently humdrum life as an official, bound by red-tape, of the Prague Workmen's Accident Insurance Institution, there blazed the all-devouring passion of the great Jewish prophets' universal longing for goodness and truth.

Franz Kafka is for me one of the last, and therefore perhaps also one of the greatest, because closest to us, of mankind's religious and ethical teachers.

Kafka was the most important and fundamental experience of my youth, a bitter-sweet upheaval which brought into play all the potentialities of my self, a trauma of adolescence which, at the time when I made Kafka's acquaintance, I tried to master by making careful entries in my diary. In this way especially I preserved what he said to me. The occasions which provoked them were only very briefly and cursorily noted; they did not seem to me to be important. All I could see was *my* Kafka. He was an intellectual *feu-de-joie*. Everything else fell into shadow. This naturally also affected the language and the form of my entries, not so much in my diaries, as the special notes I made in a thick grey exercise book which I regarded as my own continuing 'Treasury of Ideas'.

In this I deposited a hybrid collection of quotations, poems, newspaper cuttings, literary plans and ideas, anecdotes and stories, incidents which had struck me and what other people had said to me, and most of all Kafka's comments on the most varied subjects and occasions. Extracted from the 'Treasury of Ideas' they might have formed a valuable collection of striking aphorisms. But this could not have been done by mechanically copying the text, because I frequently omitted to give the source and the occasion of the various comments. My 'Treasury of Ideas' was, I now see, an amorphous collection of hastily recorded scraps of reading and conversation, the origin of which I only really knew at the moment when I wrote them down.

This became clear to me when, two years after Franz Kafka's death, I stayed at Stará Ríse in the highlands of Bohemia-Moravia with Josef Florian, the Czech, orthodox Catholic publisher and publicist.

At his request, I made a selection of the entries in my diary, and from my 'Treasury of Ideas', for Florian to publish in Czech. But this never happened, because I could not make my feelings and ideas acceptable to Florian's Catholic orthodoxy.

Then there began for me a period of restless wandering between different people, towns, ideas and occupations. In the course of it, the intellectual and emotional experience of my youth was drowned by a flood of new adventures. The image of Kafka faded away. I turned away from what had been fundamental to my youth, and in doing so from my real self, from all the potentialities of my own basic nature. Just as, in my cupboard, the package containing my soberly recorded notes and reminiscences and the grey book of my 'Treasury of Ideas' lay abandoned under a pile of old notebooks, sketches, drawings and newspaper cuttings, so the images and the words of the days when I used to meet Kafka were lost in a desert of false ideas of happiness and pleasure. My mind was purified only by the pressure of war and violence. I suddenly stood face to face with the insect world of *The Metamorphosis* and the cold and merciless machinery of *In the Penal Settlement*.

My friend, the well-known Prague composer, George Vachovec, and his wife Johanna, to whom I spoke of what seemed to me this sinister transformation of the world around me, told me that my memories of Kafka did not belong to me alone.

'You must publish the conversations. You are Kafka's witness, who perhaps possess the key to his innermost being.' I replied that I was not acquainted with the full range of his work; the man I had met was not the writer, but my father's friend at the office. This made my friend's wife furious. She threw both hands in the air and cried: 'Don't you understand anything? Great writing, which has a meaning for all mankind, involves the whole of a man. That's quite clear in this case. There's no soundproof concrete wall between Franz Kafka, the lawyer, and Franz Kafka, the writer. One can hear that perfectly clearly in his conversations with you. The conversations are now a part of his work. Therefore you should not withhold them from the world.'

To this I had no reply.

I took my notes out of the mass of papers in my cupboard and gave them to my friend's wife to type because at that time, in 1947, I had, though innocent, endured nearly fourteen months' imprisonment for purposes of interrogation in Prague's notorious prison of Pankrác, and had suffered severely both in mind and body.

In a few days Jana Vachovec typed one top and two carbon copies of my manuscript, to which she added explanatory notes and references. Without consulting me, she sent the top copy from the Prague General Post Office, on 21 March 1947, to

Max Brod at Tel Aviv in Israel. But since for weeks no reply arrived, and my friend's wife was very impatient, she sent a copy to her uncle, the printer Emil Kossak, in Stockholm. But from him also there was no reply. So I decided to offer my book to a small firm of publishers in New York. I let them have, without a receipt, the last typed copy of my book – and never saw it again.

Silence. Then Christmas week of 1949 arrived, and with it a letter of 14 December 1947, in which Kafka's faithful friend and companion Max Brod expressed his opinion of my book. He drew my attention to a few small factual mistakes in the notes but otherwise praised my reminiscences as a 'good and important book, rich in information'. He would gladly use all his influence to get the book published.

I gave Max Brod the right to make any necessary changes in the book. My trust in him was dealt a shattering blow by the publication of the book, the contract for which I had not seen and the changes in which had not been shown to me. For in the published work a large part of the original text was missing, including a few passages to which I attached particular importance, because they revealed the hidden rebelliousness of the dream-intoxicated author of *The Metamorphosis* and *In the Penal Settlement*, his unconcealed hatred of bureaucracy, his groans and recurrent bitter despair in that factory of torment which was his office, his deep involvement with the history of Prague, his fantastic obsession with the ambiguous meanings of language, the sarcasm with which he stripped political bosses of their pretensions, his real insight into every kind of political illusion, his gay and macabre humour, and his severely critical attitude to the world.

All this was almost entirely missing from the printed text, which was published by Fischer in 1951. My book was a mere skeleton, a mutilated embryo, a pitiful remnant, at the sight of which my heart shrank. It was a book constricted by blinkers, a horizon diminished by omissions, a tired, tight-lipped mouth with broken teeth.

Why had Max Brod done this?

Why all the omissions from my reminiscences? To whom did they give offence?

The simplest way to have settled the matter would have been to write to Max Brod. But that was precisely what I could not do. Brod had taken trouble to get my book published, I owed him a debt of gratitude, and also – I had given him a complete power of attorney for any omissions and changes he might make. It was impossible for me now to protest. I could only hold my tongue, as they say. But for doing this I really do not have the right talent. I can only with the greatest difficulty conceal feelings of dissatisfaction. And so it was in the case of my mutilated book. It will be seen later how unjust I was in all my suspicions of Max Brod.

The mutilated book became a spiritual torment to me. I was an important witness who refused to testify.

How could I give any kind of testimony now? The type-script of the original text and the two copies were lost. I had no copy. My wife, during the time when, despite my innocence, I was in prison, had burned the diary. And the 'Treasury of Ideas'? I have no inkling where it vanished. How could I bring the past to life again?

I had been living for several months under terrible pressure, from which I could not escape. I sank more deeply under it from day to day. My wife, Helene, had died after a long and painful illness. A short time after, my daughter Anna was killed in a road crash. I was not able to attend her funeral, and I had only partly paid for the burial of my wife, as I had no money.

I was hardly ever free from sickness. And my physical collapse was accompanied by a gradual decline in my intellectual and moral strength. Gaps appeared in my hitherto remarkable memory. I lost control of mechanical manual operations and forgot quite ordinary trivial things. Life no longer seemed to me to be worthwhile. The only desire I still retained was for order. I did not want to leave behind any burden or confusion. So I went to my old home in the Nationalstrasse, which I had only rarely visited, and then only for a very short time, after my wife's death. I meant to collect and give away my remaining possessions. After a brief half an hour, a pile of miscellaneous objects stood on the table. I looked around for a suitcase, but there wasn't one in the room. I had, however, noticed a couple of old parcels lying on the bookshelves in the lavatory. So I took from there a large, dilapidated old cardboard box. It was filled with remnants of material, packets of sewing needles and faded patterns. I emptied the box on the floor. At the very bottom lay a volume of old waltzes by Johann Strauss and beneath it my old 'Treasury of Ideas'. Out of the Strauss waltzes projected a sheaf of typed papers. It was the original of the missing sections of my *Conversations with Kafka*. I had to sit down.

Max Brod has not wilfully bowdlerized my book. He had not omitted or suppressed a single paragraph. I had been unjust to him for years. The fault lay in my easy going nature, which took everything for granted. Johanna Vachovec in her well-meant impatience had simply not sent the whole of the original typescript to Max Brod. That was all that had happened. I don't know how the papers got into the Strauss score and into the box. But that isn't important any more.

So I can only begin to organize the remains of my life by completing my witness to Kafka. But this is not the end, it is only the beginning. And not only for me, but for many others.

Kafka is – as the good and faithful Brod said – a prophetic figure, and so what I wrote here as a public confession and apology is not an end but the opening of a door, a small fragment of hope, a breath of life, and so a strengthening of everything that is living and indestructible in us sinful men after all the torments of fear and disillusion which we endure.

GUSTAV JANOUCH

NOTES

*

✳

1. Max Brod made possible the beginning of Kafka's literary career, in 1912, by recommending his *Considerations* to the publishing firm of Rowohlt. Previously, in 1909, he had sent two short prose pieces to the magazine, *Hyperion*, in which they were published. – Max Brod's book, *Tycho Brache's Weg zu Gott* (Tycho Brache's Way to God), was published by Kurt Wolff in 1916, with the dedication: 'To my friend Franz Kafka.'

2. Paul Adler (1878–1946). His novel, *Die Zauberflöte* (The Magic Flute), was published in 1916.

3. Ludwig Winder (1889–1946) edited the Prague newspaper *Bohemia* until 1928. His novel, *Die jüdische Orgel* (The Jewish Organ), was published in 1922. He emigrated to Palestine shortly before Hitler came to power in Germany.

4. David Garnett's *Lady into Fox* was published in 1922.

5. Otto Pick (1887–1940), well known as a translator from Czech, was first a bank employee, later editor of the Prague newspaper, *Prager Presse*. In 1938, he emigrated to England, where he died.

6. At the time when these conversations took place, Kafka's father's warehouse was located in the Kinsky Palace on the Altstädter Ring; Kafka lived with his parents in the Oppelt House, on the corner of the Pariser Strasse and the Altstädter Ring.

7. Felix Weltsch (1884–1964), philosopher and publicist was editor-in-chief of the Prague Zionist weekly, *Selbstwehr* (Self-Defence).

8. The story *Der Heizer* (The Stoker) forms the first chapter of Franz Kafka's novel, *Amerika*.

9. Milena Jesenská (1895–1944) was Kafka's first Czech translator. For her relationship with him see *Briefe an Milena*, 1952. She died in a concentration camp.

10. F. is Felice Bauer (1887–1960), to whom Franz Kafka was twice (in 1914 and 1917) engaged. For the circumstances of the dedication, see Franz Kafka, *Briefe an Felice und andere Korrespondenz aus der Verlobungszeit* (Letters to Felice and other correspondence from the period of his engagement), 1967.

11. The poem *Pokora* (Humility) is by the Czech poet Jiří Wolker. It appeared in the IVth annual series of the literary weekly *Kmen* (The Stem) on 5 September 1920.

12. Ernst Lederer (b. 1904) wrote lyric poems, of which some appeared in the review *Jung Juda* (Young Judah). He died in a concentration camp, together with his mother, his sister and his brother.

13. *Die Aktion* (Action). Weekly journal of Politics, Literature and Art. Edited by Franz Pfempfert.

14. Theodor Tagger (pseudonym, Ferdinand Bruckner) (1891–1958) in 1925 founded the Renaissance Theatre in Berlin; director until 1927, he emigrated in 1933.

15. The book was a volume of the magazine-anthology *Nova et Vetera*, which appeared at irregular intervals and was published by Josef Florian in Stará Říse. Later it published the first portrait of Kafka, a woodcut by Votlucka, and the first Czech translations of his story *Die Verwandlung* (The Metamorphosis).

16. The book was the famous anthology of expressionist poetry, *Menschheitsdammerung. Symphonie jüngster Dichtung* (The Twilight of Mankind. Symphony of Contemporary Poetry), edited by Kurt Pinthus (1919).

17. The reference is to the one-act play, *Der Retter* (The Saviour) by Walter Hasenclever, and *Der grüne Kakadu* (The Green Cockatoo) by Arthur Schnitzler.

18. Walter Hasenclever's play *Der Sohn* (The Son) was well known in 1920 and later as an example of German expressionist drama.

19. Rudolf Schildkraut (1862–1950), one of the greatest German actors, who encouraged the production of plays by contemporary Yiddish authors on the Viennese, Hamburg and New York stage.

20. For Franz Kafka's relationship to the Yiddish theatrical company, see Franz Kafka, *Tagebücher* (Diaries), *Briefe an Felice* (Letters to Felice), and Max Brod, *Franz Kafka*.

21. Ernst Weiss (1884–1940), doctor and writer. He committed suicide in Paris, when the Germans occupied the city.

22. Henri Barbusse (1874–1935), French writer and socialist, author of *Le Feu* (1916) and *Clarté* (1918).

23. Kasimir Edschmid (pseudonym of Eduard Schmidt), *Die Doppelköpfige Nymphe. Aufsätze uber die Literatur und die Gegenwart* (The Two-Headed Nymph. Essays on Literature and the Present Day), 1920. Kafka is mentioned in the second chapter, *Däubler ind die Schule der Abstrakten* (Däubler and the Abstract School).

24. Johannes Urzidil (b. 1896) was Press Attaché at the German Embassy in Prague. He wrote poems and essays on culture and politics. He emigrated to the United States.

25. Lydia Holzner owned and directed a private school in Prague II, Pořič No. 4. Her house was a meeting place for German, Czech and foreign

writers, painters, sculptors and musicians. Lydia Holzner's brother, Dr Karl Holzner, was tutor to the young Franz Werfel.

26. Leon Bloy, *Le sang du pauvre*. 1909. The Czech translation by Josef Florian appeared in 1911 – Leon Bloy, *Le salut par les Juifs*. 1892.

27. Carl Dallago (1869–1949), lyric poet and philosopher; he was a member of Ludwig von Ficker's Brenner circle. His *Der Christ Kierkegaards* (Kierkegaard's Christ) was published in 1922.

28. Hans Klaus, Hans Tine Kanton (Konstantin Ahne) and Rudolf Altschul in November 1920 organized a lecture evening in the Mozarteum in Prague. The introductory speech was made by Otto Pick, who hastened to explain that *Der Protest* (Protest) was not the name of a literary group. The star speaker of the evening was Otto Soltau, a member of the Prague *Deutsches Theater* who had won the admiration of the organizers of the meeting by his performance as Hasenclever's *Der Sohn* – Konstantin Ahne in 1920 published under the name of Hans Tine Kanton a book of poems, *Leben – Nebel* (Life – Fog). Stories and poems by Hans Klaus appeared in various newspapers and magazines; in 1930 a play by him was given its first performance in the *Neue Deutsche Theater* in Prague – Rudolf Altschul was well known as a distinguished Prague nerve specialist.

29. Johannes Robert Becher (1891–1958), poet, dramatist, novelist and essayist. His poem, *An den Schlaf* (To Sleep), was published in the *Insel-Almanach*, 1918.

30. Albert Ehrenstein, *Tubutsch*, with twelve drawings by Oskar Kokoschka. 1919. – The book, *Der Mensch Schreit* (Humanity Screams), mentioned by Kafka, was published in 1916.

31. Johannes Schlaf, *Frühling* (Spring) – Insel Bücherei No. 49. – The geocentric problems preoccupied Johannes Schlaf for many years. His first published book on the subject appeared in 1914: *Professor Plassmann und das Sonnenfleckenphänomen* (Professor Plassmann and the Phenomenon of Sunspots), Leipzig: Hephaistos-Verlag. – His most important works on the subject were: *Die geocentrische Tatsache als unmittelbare Folgerung aus den Sonnenfleckphänomen* (The fact of Geocentricism as a Direct Consequence of the Phenomenon of Sunspots), Leipzig: R. Hummel 1925; and: *Kosmos und Kosmischer Umlauf. Die geozentriche Lösung des kosmischen Problems* (Cosmos and Cosmic rotation. The Geocentric Solution of the Cosmic Problem), 1927.

32. *Die Bhagavad Gita. Das Hohe Lied, enthaltend die Lehre der Unsterblichkeit* (The Bhagavad Gita. The High Song, containing the Doctrine of Immortality). In metrical form done into German from Edwin Arnold's translation from the Sanskrit by Franz Hartmann, M.D.

33. The reference is to the volume of poems *Prichazim z pereiferie* (I come from the Periphery) by Michael Mareš, privately printed in 1920.

34. The Altstädter Kaffeehaus was once a well-known night club at the top of the Ekidigasse. It was closed down in the 1920s.

35. At the beginning of the twentieth century the public house, *Zum Kanonen-kreuz*, was a well-known anarchist meeting place, and in 1910 it played an important part in the trial of the Czech pacifist League of Youth. Max Brod, who together with Franz Kafka frequented the anarchist meetings in the public house, has preserved its atmosphere in his novel *Stefan Rott oder Das Jahr der Entscheidung* (Stefan Rott, or The Year of Decision). In it, he mentioned many of the participants by their real names; among them, Michael Mareš, whose reminiscences of Kafka's part in the Prague anarchist movements were printed by Klaus Wagenbach in 1958 in his book *Franz Kafka – eine Biographie seiner Jugend* (Franz Kafka – a biography of his Youth).

36. Erich Mühsam (1878–1934), socialist poet, dramatist and essayist.

37. Arthur Holitscher (1869–1941), impressioniss novelist, dramatist and essayist.

38. Oskar Baum (1883–1941) went blind early in life and made his livelihood as a teacher of music. His writings were deeply autobiographical: *Uferdasein. Aus dem Blindeleben* (Living on the Bank. A Blind Man's Life) Stuttgart-Berlin, Axel Juncker; *Das Leben ist Dunkel* (Life in Darkness), 1909; in addition, *Die Tür ins Unmögliche* (The Door to the Impossible), 1919. His play *Das Wunder* (The Miracle) received its first performance in Prague in 1920.

39. Karl Kraus (b. 1874), published the magazine, *Die Fackel* (The Touch), written entirely by himself, in Vienna from 1899 to 1934. He died in 1936.

40. In his *Blätter des Burgtheaters* (Burgtheater Papers), George Kulka published under his own name, with very little alteration, an extract from Jean Paul's *Vorschule der Aesthetik* (Prolegomena to Aesthetics).

41. Alfred Polgar (1875–1955), essayist and critic.

42. The reference is to *Die Gebete der Demut* (Prayers of Humility), a selection and translation of Francis Jammes's poetry by Ernst Stadler, which was published in 1913 by Kurt Wolff as a volume in the collection *Der Jüngste Tag* (Day of Judgement).

43. Alfred Döblin (1878–1957), novelist, dramatist and essayist. In 1915 and 1919 he published his two novels, *Die Drei Sprünge des Wang-Lun* (The Three Leaps of Wang-Lun) and *Der Schwarze Vorhang* (The Black Curtain).

44. Alfred Döblin, *Die Ermordung einer Butterblume und anderere Erzählungen* (Murder of a Buttercup and other Stories), 1913.

45. Franz Blei (1871–1942), founder and sometime editor of literary and biblio-phile journals, and translator.

46. Michael Grusemann, *Dostojewski*. Philosophische Reihe 28. Edited by Dr Alfred Werner, 1921.

47. Leo Frobenius (ed.), *Atlantis. Volksmärchen und Volksdichtungen Afrikas* (Atlantis. Tribal Fairy Stories and Poetry from Africa). Published by the Research Institute for Cultural Morphology, Munich, and printed by Eugen Diedrichs, Jena. 12 vols. (1921–1928).

48. Leonhard Frank's collection of stories, *Der Mensch ist gut* (Man is Good), published (1918) by Rascher in Zürich and Leipzig before the end of the First World War, became a manifesto of the post-war pacifist movement in Germany.

49. Ludwig Hardt (1886–1947).

50. The poet Rudolf Fuchs (b. 1890) was one of the leading figures in the Prague publishing firm of H. Mercy, which published the well-known middle-class liberal newspaper *Prager Tagblatt*. He published his first book of poems, *Meteor*, in 1913. His collection of poems, *Die Karawane* (The Caravan), was published by Kurt Wolff in Leipzig in 1918, where he also published his translations and adaptations of the poems of Otokar Březina and Petr Bezruč.

51. Alexander Neverov, *Taschkent, die Brotreiche Stadt* (Tashkent, the Bountiful City). The German translation was published in 1921.

52. *Poale Zion* (Workers of Zion) was the name of the Jewish workers' party within the Zionist movement. It originated in Poland and Russia as an attempted synthesis of Zionism with social democracy.

53. The reference is to the collection edited by Artur Landsberger: *Das Ghettobuch. Die Schönsten Geschichte aus dem Ghetto* (The Ghetto Book. The Most Beautiful Stories from the Ghetto), 1921.

54. Dr Karel Kramář (1860-1937) in 1894 became a Member of Parliament of the Young Czech party. After the collapse of the Austro-Hungarian empire in 1918 he became the first Minister-President of Czechoslovakia. Dr Karel Kramář was the acknowledged leader of the Czech nationalists, who were united in the former National Democratic Party. As such, he was an outspoken opponent of Thomas G. Masaryk and Dr Edvard Beneš.

55. Odradek is the name of a creature who appears in Kafka's short stories, *Die Sorge des Hausvaters* (Anxieties of a Paterfamilias), in his book *Ein Landarzt* (A Country Doctor). – See also (Note 26) the previously mentioned book by Leon Bloy, *Le salut par les Juifs*.

56. The 'Society of Marxist Academicians' in Prague was a social democratic association which after the split in the party became affiliated to the Communists. – The so-called *Rosa-Saal* was a medium-sized lecture-room in the social democratic House of the People, *Lidový dum*, in Prague II, Hybernergasse.

57. *Die Befreiung der Menschheit. Freiheitsideen in Vergangenheit und Gegenwart* (The Liberation of Mankind. Ideas of Freedom in Past and Present), edited by Ignaz Jezower (1921).

58. Kafka admired Vincent van Gogh's picture *Le Café, le Soir*, Arles, September 1888, which is in the Rijkmuseum Kröller-Müller in Otterlo.

59. The reference is to the jubilee number of the illustrated weekly, *Wiener Bilder*.

60. The news sheet *Očista* (The Clarification), written and published from 1919 to 1920 by A. V. Fric, attacked the then Foreign Minister, Edvard Beneš.

After the foundation of the Czechoslovak Republic Fric wished to become ambassador to Mexico. Dr Beneš did not respond to his suggestion and thus provoked Fric's attacks.

61. Franz Kafka's memorandum on the reorganization of the Workmen's Accident Insurance Institution of the Kingdom of Bohemia is to be found in the Institution's archives.

62. *Franz Werfel, Spiegelmensch* (Mirror Man). A magic trilogy, 1920.

63. Franz Werfel's novel about music, to which Kafka refers, was finally published as *Verdi. Roman der Oper* (Verdi. A Novel of the Opera), 1924.

64. Johannes Bühler (ed.), *Was sich Wüstenväter und Mönche erzählten* (Tales the Desert Fathers and Monks Told), 1919.

65. Vítězslav Novák (1870–1949) was one of the leading figures in modern music. Max Brod strongly and successfully encouraged public acceptance of the music both of Vitezslav Novák and of Leo Janacek.

66. *Naše Reč* (Our Language) was the title of a journal devoted to the study of the Czech language. Its editor-in-chief was Prof. Dr Miroslav Haller.

67. The reference is to *Menschheitsdämmerung*, see Note 16.

68. Rudolf Steiner (1861–1925), founder of anthroposophy, occasionally visited Prague where he was supported and encouraged by various German-Jewish societies and families.

69. George Grosz, *Das Gesicht der herrschenden Klasse* (The Face of the Ruling Class).

70. Vladimír Sychra (b. 1903), one of the most important of the modern Czech painters who form the *Manes* group. He is a professor at the Academy of Plastic Art.

71. The series of works of the ancient Chinese thinkers published by Eugen Diedrichs in Jena was a ten-volume collection of original texts translated and edited by the German sinologist Richard Wilhelm-Tsingtau. They included the most important works of classical religion and philosophy, medieval political and natural science, and Taoism and its various sects.

72. Josef Čapek (1887–1945) who wrote many successful books in collaboration with his brother Karel Čapek (1890–1938). He was primarily, however, a painter of original talent, who founded the *Tvrdosijni* (Die-hard) group.

73. Giovanni Segantini (1858–1899) was a distinguished Alpine painter. The volume referred to of *Schriften und Briefe* (Letters and Writings) was edited by his widow.

74. Guillaume Apollinaire, *Alcools. Poèmes 1898–1913*. Paris: Mercure de France, 1913. Karel Čapek's translation appeared in the Prague journal, *Cerven*, on 6 February 1919.

75. Max Brod, *Heidentum, Christentum, Judentum* (Paganism, Christianity, Judaism), was published in 1922.

76. Oscar Wilde: *Ziele* (Intentions), translated by Paul Wertheimer, 1918.

77. *Prince Kuckuck. Leben, Taten, Meinungen und Höllenfahrt eines Wohllüstlings. In einem Zeitroman* (Prince Cuckoo. Life, Adventures, Opinions and Descent into Hell of a Debauchee. In a Novel of our own Times) by Otto Julius Bierbaum. 3 vols. (1906–1907).

78. Franz Kafka expressed his admiration for Charles Dickens on a number of occasions. Unfortunately, I have not preserved all his comments on this subject.

79. Franz Kafka is buried in the Jewish cemetery in Prague-Straschnitz, together with his father, Hermann Kafka (1854–1931), and his mother, Julie Kafka *née* Löwy (1858–1934).

INDEX

New Directions Paperbooks—A Partial Listing

For complete listing request complete catalog from
New Directions, 80 Eighth Avenue, New York 10011

† Bilingual